MW01264633

# JOURNEY TO ULTIMATE SPIRITUALITY

## Jackie Woods

Adawehi Press
P.O. Box 1549
Columbus, North Carolina 28722
www.adawehi.com

Printed in the United States of America

Library of Congress Catalogue Card Number: 00-091297

ISBN: 0-9659665-2-6

# Acknowledgements

This book was made possible by the continued commitment and loving support of my students on their journey to ultimate spirituality.

I also want to give a special acknowledgement to Terri Morrin for her help in getting this book ready for print.

Thank you to all of you readers who join me now in synergy.

# Contents

# Preface

For twenty plus years Jackie Woods has taught people to listen to their hearts for guidance. She has had them practice listening to all the bodies – physical, emotional, mental, and spiritual – so they could discern when the spiritual was speaking. She taught how the mental, emotional, and physical bodies work together to support the spiritual. She would take individual heart qualities, such as Acceptance, Discernment, Balance, etc. and get to know them as you would a good friend. She has been a guide on the path to spirituality for thousands of people.

At first Jackie's work was done only through private sessions but when she started supplementing students' private work with classes the results became logarithmic. Even with just a small synergy of twelve people, the effect was dramatic. It became obvious that if a synergy of twelve could increase the rate of an individual's growth perceptively, then stepping up the numbers of the synergy would be an even greater support. Jackie then experimented with joining all one hundred of her current students together through the synergy of community. It is working.

Her next step has been to write this book in order to teach more people how to tap into the larger, universal synergy. As you learn how to be in synergy with a few, you can then take the next step and become part of all hearts that have chosen a spiritual path.

> *It is from this place of universal synergy that ultimate spirituality is found. You cannot get there alone.*

Exercises have been included in this book that will support you on your journey to ultimate spirituality. Please take them seriously. It would be helpful to get several friends together and form a study group. As you need further help, Jackie teaches Internet classes that you can enroll in through the Adawehi web site, (www.adawehi.com).

In this book Jackie has compiled six workshops which she has given at various times. Two explain the subject of synergy. Two introduce the importance of heart qualities. These were included because the heart is the key to the door of synergy. Two show how a heart quality (the one chosen was Discernment) can be used in the four bodies correctly so that synergy can be a part of both our growth and manifestation cycles. This added ingredient of synergy will not only increase growth on the planet but will change the structures of society. It is only through synergy that we can experience ultimate spirituality.

This book contains advanced concepts. If you are still struggling with questions like: What is growth and/or manifestation? What are heart qualities? How can everything be energy? Do I really create my own reality?, then you need to go back and read the companion to this book, <u>Spiritual Energy Cycles</u>. If, however, you have already read that book or consider yourself to be well grounded in metaphysical principles, then read on!

Since synergy is the key to ultimate Spirituality, this book jumps right into the subject of synergy in to shed some light on

1. What synergy is,
2. Why it is such a worthwhile goal, and
3. Give you some exercises to help you see where you fit into all of this.

The first part may seem like very intense reading. Don't despair! After you have been tempted with the "fabulous prizes" that you stand to gain, the book will downshift in Part II and go back to the beginning to spell everything out. You will be taken step by step through the process of "tuning up" your physical, emotional, mental, and spiritual bodies so that you can resonate from the heart and enter into synergy.

In presenting the material this way, you will be ready to look again at synergy with much deeper understanding by the time you reach Synergy II in chapter four. The final two chapters on Discernment will help this synergy from being blocked on its way into your world.

Not only have exercises been offered at the end of each chapter, but also a group discussion section has been offered for those who are ready to go further. These discussions may need to wait until you have digested, or internalized, the concepts offered in the exercises. It probably would serve you well to read the book twice. Happy journeying!

# 1

# Synergy

I am sure all of you have experienced those wonderful "heart moments". Those times when you feel nothing can harm you, when nothing is beyond your reach. It is in those moments that you can forgive, accept, and reconcile. A "heart moment" happens when you have absolute clarity about what is going on inside of you and around you. Actually the "heart moment" may last several hours or on rare occasions, days. Those are the times when your heart is in charge, clearly directing the mind, emotions, and physical world. You can move forward or patiently wait. All is right.

Because most of us seek and long for a heart directed life, but lack the will power to stay focused on that intent, this book introduces you to synergy. The word synergy is thrown around a lot these days, but it is not generally used to its fullest meaning. The full scope of synergy goes as far as you are willing to let your heart go.

If you can resonate with a small group and have synergy, why not take it up a notch and resonate with all the people on the planet who are being their true essence, or being in their heart. This high level of vibration not only gives you more of what you need, but also provides the support to maintain a heart space. This is the type of synergy that will be talked about in this book.

Being in a heart space simply means you are allowing one of the qualities of the heart to be present in you. All the qualities of the heart are available to you but not all are claimed. For instance, Patience is a quality of the heart that is often times claimed by mothers. To be a good friend you need to claim such heart qualities as Kindness, Gentleness, Clarity, and sometimes you may even need Strength. The list of heart qualities is almost endless. (Several are listed at the end of the book.)

The purpose of our life here on earth is to claim these qualities as our own. They are our birthright, our gifts from God. Once we claim them, we can empower them through expression.

Let's go back to the example of Patience. You can claim it and allow it to become strong in you. It is however in expressing Patience, because you have claimed it as yours, that you resonate with others who also have claimed Patience. You then have stepped into synergy, and Patience has become big. It is like having Patience flow from you and join with all the Patience in the world.

What is the difference between strong and big? Strong means you can access a particular heart quality well, while big means you are that heart quality. It has become part of your repertoire. You don't have to reclaim it every time you use it. There is now a permanent space for that energy in your being because you have joined it in the big God space of synergy. You now don't just borrow Patience by bringing it into your small space to use. You become a part of that particular heart quality in the whole universe.

## ♥ *The Powerful vs. Non-powerful Person*

How will synergy affect your day to day life? Let's start by looking at what characteristics differentiate a powerful person from a non-powerful person. If you will observe closely you will discover the non-powerful person expresses without resonance. They speak only from themselves. They may express with confidence and even realness but there is nothing more than them. Now I am not saying they don't share emotional experiences with their friends, they many times do. They also can work side by side and get a lot done. They may have stimulating even titillating conversations, but they stand alone. The non-powerful person doesn't resonate with anyone else. Life doesn't fill them up and life doesn't flow through them.

Whereas the powerful person doesn't have to say or do a lot for you to feel their very life force lift you up when you are around them. Doors in life seem to open for them. This isn't to say they are always money rich or emotionally 'up'. Powerful people have to be in the growth process like everybody else. So what makes the difference? As has been stated before, it is the resonance. The powerful person is connected to and resonating from, a bigger, more powerful space than the non-powerful person.

Where does this resonance come from? It comes from the joining together of all hearts – the hearts of the spiritual masters, the angels, and all the light beings of earth who share heart qualities. All get to join together on a vibratory energy wave that resonates across the planet.

Yet, why are there so few truly powerful people in the world?

*Few people have recognized the Power of their heart.*

The minute you claim and own a heart quality you have the capacity to plug into a group resonance. You have a standing invitation to become part of a spirit synergy. This synergy is made up of all people who have defined themselves as being heart qualities. How can you stay in resonance with all those that have reached that particular level of heart vibration? The key is to give up being separate.

We have so identified who we are with our programmed patterns of thinking, feeling, and behaving, that we fear losing ourselves if we merge with other hearts. We inherently know that giving ourselves over to a synergy, something bigger than our present space, will change us. It is our fear that tells us we will lose our individuality. Synergy is an expansive, powerful force that stands alone holding universal Power, Love and Wisdom and all the heart qualities that fit under those main headings. Even though synergy is a separate force, it is not about separation. It unifies us all and at the same time empowers our individualized God selves. We have our individual place with each heart quality we become. What we try to hold on to when we claim separateness is our ego self. The ego can never be unified or synergized because the ego cannot be part of all hearts.

Synergy, as a single force, is hard to comprehend because we have experienced life mostly from a small space that was about us personally, or about another person, or about two or more people doing something together. In none of these spaces were our energies merged. We may have gone away from the interaction with a certain satisfaction, but without knowing we were one. We were not bigger, we were not more powerful, nor were we in synergy.

Doing activities with other people doesn't create synergy. But, being around others may help make you aware of a longing to connect to people in a deeper more significant way. It is that longing, however, that sometimes leads us down a dead end path that results in attachment to forms of expression rather than identification with the heart energy expressed. For instance, if you put a lot of energy into getting the people at your job to like you, this may give you a sense of external acceptance but you still may not know that you have Acceptance as part of you. This of course leads down the road marked non-powerful. You will cling to the form of smiling and speaking even if it isn't coming from your heart. If, however, being with those people brings you into an appreciation of their "innerness" and your own real self, then being around those people helps you to choose synergy.

You can walk into an area and feel the unity when people are working together from a place of synergy. You don't have to talk; just be there. Being there for the same inner purpose helps to create a synergy where all are one, all are more. It isn't about the level of skill, what people are wearing, or what they own. It is about resonating together from a higher vibration. People in synergy can leave the group, go home, and be powerful because they have become more than themselves - a synergy. That is until they let life once again define them as separate.

Did you ever feel you were being pulled apart? On the outside the business of life is pulling you, and on the inside, your longing to belong, to connect, is pulling you. Unfortunately many of us prefer to keep these two areas separate. When we look inside we see only ourselves. We don't see or feel everyone else who is looking inside. We are afraid to step out of our small separate space and join synergy. We don't see or feel all the regular people, the Angels, and the Masters, that have already looked inside and seen everyone else. We only see ourselves so how are we to know and believe in what we can't see or feel? How are we to believe that synergy exists? Each time we look and see only ourselves our fear is reinforced rather than our Power. This is the way of the non-powerful person. We are powerless to take care of our need to be more, or any other need for that matter. By not being able to meet our needs, (which are always energies of the bigger heart space), we feel powerless. This in turn keeps us feeling too inadequate to connect to anything bigger, like synergy. Thus the powerless cycle continues.

It is pretty scary to face life feeling powerless so we devise schemes to look powerful in order to throw everyone off. We do good work not for the purpose of expressing our heart, but to prove how capable or "powerful" we are. We develop a charming personality in hopes that someone will take note of how wonderful we are. We dress in our own personal style to make a mark, our mark, in our own personal world. We have sex, we please, we confront, none of which makes us powerful. We can feel like we have some control and everything is a little less scary and we may even convince ourselves that we are powerful.

You don't have to see your life as powerless and pathetic. There is another road: one of true Power, one that really works.

### ♥ *Giving and Receiving - Powerfully*

Giving and Receiving can be a universal energy exchange or it can be a token substitute for the real thing. The first way is the way of a powerful person. The second is the way of the non-powerful.

So many people express from non-powerful spaces that it is hard to receive much if we stay in their small exchange space. However, the powerful person stands in a doorway to the bigger world of spirit. If your choice has been to live in that world and be a part of that synergy then you can step through the doorway even if the other person doesn't step through. You can receive as much as you can resonate. It is like taking one little sound and letting it echo in a big cathedral. A small gift can be taken into your heart when you are a powerful person and be multiplied. In your space there is no lack.

The same applies when you give as a powerful person. The one you are giving to often has only a small receiving space because they haven't yet chosen to be part of synergy. As a powerful person you not only receive for all of synergy, but you also give from all of synergy. Get this picture; the powerful person is pouring a whole pitcher of water into a little juice glass. This seems rather stupid doesn't it? Well then let's add another piece to the picture. The water that doesn't fit into the glass can spill onto the ground and become part of the whole again. This is the way it is when we live from the synergy of spirit; there is no waste, only Abundance. From this place of Power, giving and receiving have no boundaries. You can be as big as you choose. You can be as Abundant as you choose.

> *For you to give and receive from synergy you must realize that all your needs are met as gifts from the heart.*

If for example, you need Courage, then you must call on what little Courage you have, let it resonate with the Courage of the spirit world, and presto, it is big and powerful. You are then giving and receiving to and from synergy. On the other hand, if you forget that the need you have for Courage is met by your own heart, you will probably fall victim to the standard barter system that says I will take care of you and you take care of me. This kind of exchange has no resonance and no Power.

> *The powerful person has found that we live first in a world of energy and secondly in a world of forms.*

When you are powerful you are aware from your experience of synergy that the universal heart energies not only meet the needs of your individual heart, but also create the physical forms you emotionally and mentally want. If ever since childhood you have wanted more Love, then you must first go to your own heart and claim whatever Love you have there. Take that Love, no matter how small, to the universal synergy of Love to be amplified and you will find that your heart will be ecstatic with its long lost treasure. However, the power of synergy doesn't end there. It then helps your mind to redefine and clarify, because your needy mind wanted someone else to come love you. Now you no longer need Love to come to you but to be shared by you. Your mind can now decide how you want to share your Love. Your emotions are no longer waiting for someone to love you, and are instead celebrating the gift you have to share. The person you create to be in relationship with will be quite different now that you are a synergy person, because you will have created from Power not weakness. You will have created from a filled place not an empty one.

When you are a non-powerful person you can receive but

since you are not part of a bigger resonating group, you usually do what is called hoarding. You take whatever is being offered and try to hold on to it because the gift can only be as big as your small space can receive. As a result, you feel needy and in lack much of the time, thus the need to hoard. The giver will get nothing back from you, because immediate exchange can only happen with the resonance of synergy. This is not to say as a non-powerful person you don't give, you do, but your gift is often taken lightly since it has no Power of resonance behind it.

As a non-powerful person you can also create. You are creating all of the time, but it might not be what you want. Instead, it could be what you fear. Even if your creation is not from fear, but a creation from the good that is within you, you can only create to the size of your individual space. This size may not be big enough to create as much as you want. Do you realize that you have a choice about the size of your creation? You do.

CR

*As a powerful person*

*you not only*

*receive for all*

*of synergy,*

*but you also give*

*from all of synergy.*

છ

## *Exercises*

1. How do you create (powerfully or non-powerfully)?

_____

_____

_____

_____

_____

_____

2. What does it mean to give from all the synergy of spirit?

_____

_____

_____

_____

3. What does it mean to receive for all the synergy of spirit?

_____

_____

_____

_____

_____

4. What motivates your giving?

_____

_____

_____

_____

_____

_____

_____

5. What would it take for you to turn your daily decisions over to a spirit synergy?

_____

_____

_____

_____

_____

_____

_____

_____

## ♥ *Faith and Trust*

If the real road to Power is about looking inside and seeing and/or feeling everyone else who is looking inside, then how do we do it? Faith and Trust are two key components. We must let Faith connect us to the whole and then Trust that the whole, or synergy, will flow through us into our world of expression. People have said to me for years, "I wish I could be psychic like you so I could believe in the world of spirit". Actually it works the other way around. Having Faith that you are a part of that world makes you psychic. Faith is step one. Without Faith you borrow heart qualities, you don't become them.

Trust is the next necessary step. You may meditate everyday and touch the world of spirit, but without Trust it won't flow into your everyday life. You can't just leave your heart "over there," and come back to earth, so to speak, and be powerful. Synergy is about becoming part of the world of spirit, not just visiting. Once you have joined this "Power Club" then you will want to let your synergy-self express into the physical world. The expression part requires Trust.

It is a cycle, a flow. Without Faith you don't make it to spirit, without Trust you don't make it into the world. Both are vitally important to each other. Obviously you can't express from synergy until you make the connection, but blocking expression from a bigger space is like having an arm that you keep immobilized. It becomes useless. There is really no reason to have an arm if it is not useable.

> *Faith is paying homage to the sacred female.*
> *Trust is paying homage to the sacred male.*

Both the female and male aspects of God are synergistic. This simply means that all your receiving (female) aspects of the heart and all your giving (male) aspects of the heart, when resonating with those same aspects in the universe, become the universal sacred female and the universal sacred male. The female aspects of the heart, such as Acceptance and Honor allow you to feel good about yourself. The male aspects of the heart are what we use to be a part of the world around us, such as Courage and Strength. Actually it is not so much *what* heart energy is used as *how* it is used that determines its "gender".

Faith takes you to the sacred female to be held. Faith is letting her talk to you and instruct you. It is honoring her Love and guidance above all other Love or guidance. It is the knowing that the Love, Wisdom and Power of the sacred female are all at your disposal.

Trust is allowing the sacred male to support you in your daily life. It is letting him bring you nice gifts. It is honoring his working in your life more than you honor the empty forms. It is realizing that his magnetism is much more powerful than all your manipulation and forcing. The sacred male will literally pull the forms that you need to you. His Wisdom will know which forms are best and his Love will insure that no one will be run over or misused in the process. Trust in him makes all this happen. It is so simple that you may miss it. All you have to do is to turn loose of fear and detach from all the forms that hold your fears in place, then choose Faith and then choose Trust. If you do it step by step, day by day, it is quite easy.

> *When you choose to resonate with universal Faith and Trust, you automatically enter the door to universal synergy.*

Your needs merge with those of the whole and your expression serves the whole. You are no longer in a self-centered, small space. You are big; you are powerful. With that increased Power and space you are able to see beyond your tiny need to the bigger picture. In the bigger picture your needs don't get lost they get clarified. The "you" doesn't get destroyed; it gets redefined and empowered.

Needs and heart energies are one and the same. Every need, if carried as a heart quality by Faith to synergy, and then carried by Trust into manifestation, will give you exactly what suits you best in your physical world.

For example, a friend of mine was treated with disrespect at her work for years. In fact, she experienced dishonor most of her career. No matter how much she contributed her work either went unnoticed or it was ridiculed. She knew that she wanted to be honored but it just wasn't happening. To break the cycle of dishonor she began to call for whatever little amount of Honor was available in her heart. She did this through meditation. She connected with the Honor in her heart and wrapped it in Faith. Her Honor began to resonate with the Honor of the universal whole.

She now carries Honor with her and she is no longer bothered by her fellow employee's lack of Honor. She isn't attached to receiving praise from them. She no longer tries to *get* Honor from others, Honor is *within* her.

But that's not the end of it. She yearned for more. It felt good to carry the energy of Honor, but she wanted to experience Honor in her physical world. Time for Trust to enter the picture. My friend called on the energy of Trust in her meditation and then began to not only make things manifest, but began to guide the happenings in the most perfect way. To that end, several fellow employees began to take note of her accomplishments. Her expression of Trust has now been fully claimed by her - from her heart and into her world.

> *Faith expands what heart energies you have so that you feel better and Trust puts them into physical forms so you have more.*

We all want to feel better and have more. So what is the problem? Why isn't everyone living in synergy? Our fears tell us that this is as good as it gets unless we work harder or become a better person. They say that the best we can hope for is to use Faith and Trust to make our little world better. Maybe the God of the universe will drop us a few special favors if we pray diligently enough. Fear says that we can't possibly be part of the energy of God; we can't be part of a big synergy. It says we aren't ready! Fear lies.

If Faith and Trust work for you in your separateness, why not use them to take yourself to synergy, i.e., to the universal sacred female and male? It is from synergy that you affect the whole consciousness of the planet. Through synergy you can be powerful enough to create way beyond your own little drama; while at the same time improve and enlarge your own little world.

The magnitude of *who you are* is so great that your vision has never seen there, your imagination has never gone there, and your heart has never known full celebration.

## *Exercises*

1. How is Faith and Trust different?

_____

_____

_____

_____

_____

_____

_____

2. What does it mean to Honor the sacred female in all of life?

_____

_____

_____

_____

_____

_____

_____

_____

_____

_____

3. What does it mean to Honor the sacred male in all of life?

_____

_____

_____

_____

_____

_____

4. How can your needs fit into the big picture without getting swallowed up?

_____

_____

_____

_____

_____

_____

_____

_____

_____

_____

_____

5. How does the "you" get redefined and empowered by becoming one with the universal synergy?

_____

_____

_____

_____

_____

_____

_____

_____

_____

_____

_____

_____

_____

_____

_____

_____

_____

_____

_____

CR

*It is from*

*synergy*

*that you affect*

*the whole consciousness*

*of*

*the planet.*

BO

♥ *From Synergy to Mission*

When you become part of the world of spirit, when you see and/or feel everyone else who is looking inside, you are ready to be on mission. I am not talking about one's "life mission" to work in a certain profession. I am referring to the agreement that you made before you came into this life, the mission you agreed to express.

> *Your mission is your physical manifestation of spiritual energy.*

Your mission will fall under one of the seven universal synergy-missions. Each of these seven universal synergy-missions are made up of a group of etheric angels, masters, spirit guides, and all the earth people who look inside and know they are part of the bigger picture.

The essence or purpose of these missions is:

1. To facilitate Expression of the real.
2. To live Consciously in the world.
3. To illuminate the Truth.
4. To give Birth to the God within.
5. To administer divine Transformation.
6. To deal Creatively with the world.
7. To bring Inspiration to the world.

(These seven missions will be explained under the last section of this chapter, "Your Mission".)

The overall goal of God's plan is to bring our planetary consciousness to a higher vibration, to a oneness in synergy that connects all seven synergies. The physical manifestation of that would be each of us working together around various common purposes that resonate with these seven universal missions. You may connect with one mission for a whole lifetime or you may work with several. To stand alone, outside of synergy, is not only frustrating it is ineffectual.

Mission is almost synonymous with synergy because once you are in synergy, that synergy will need to express. Energy is a moving thing and energy (on any level) loses its vitality if it can't move. Mission not only expresses, but also creates situations where more heart energies can be birthed, and the cycle continues. Just as each individual heart quality needs to express to be empowered, so does the universal synergy need to express because it is Power! We have simply moved from the microcosm to the macrocosm - from the individual pieces to the group pieces.

Once you accept that you are part of a spiritual synergy and begin to live your life from that place of Power, then your desire to express as a group synergy in the world will be foremost in your life. This new found group Power is connected by and expressed through a group mission.

You do not have to join a physical group because you are no longer an individual expressing. You as a synergy person are a group! Everyone is called by one of the seven spirit groups to work together in serving this planet.

> *When you are anti-synergy and anti-mission*
> *you are actually working against the whole*
> *universal system of healing the planet.*

Synergy without mission is like a musician without an instrument. The music gets locked inside with no way to express. Mission is simply the male aspect of the female synergy. It is the instrument that helps us express in the world. To live *in* the energies of the heart and not *from* the energies of the heart is to live in imbalance. It would mean we were all female with no male expression. Nothing would happen in our life, or in the world for that matter, if all others lived in the same inner imbalance. We would search everywhere for someone to be the male balance outside of us.

The same is true when we try to be on mission and express in the world without first claiming our strong female. We are also out of balance. We bring small gifts and usually try to make up the lack of Power in our gifts by more effort. The male and the female must work together. To separate our heart from synergy means it can only express in and for our separate little world. The female individual heart must be part of synergy in order for the male to accomplish anything of worth. So why not experience life on a bigger scale and live from the synergistic sacred female and synergistic sacred male? When we make this choice, we are on mission. We have chosen to be in Balance as part of the whole. We then care about the whole. We are no longer separate and selfish.

To claim your sacred female and be part of synergy, you must choose to live in the world of spirit. You can't just come visit occasionally. You have to move in to that world. Once you have moved in, the energy of all sacred females is yours. You are no longer alone and lonely. You are no longer insecure about who you are. You are no longer inadequate. You feel full and content but only temporarily. Energy is always moving. It stands to reason that if you are more energy you will feel a more urgent need to let it move and flow into the world as expression.

You are now faced with another decision. You must choose to take the spirit world synergy into the physical world. Having made that decision, you have at your disposal the energy of all sacred males to help you in your expression. You no longer waffle in indecision. You no longer lack direction. You no longer have to push. It really doesn't seem like much of a choice but it does require a choice.

Why would anyone choose to stay in separation and not be on mission? (By the way, you cannot be on mission outside of synergy.) It makes no difference how many good deeds you do or how many certificates you hang on your wall, you are not on mission by yourself. Yet many of us hold on to "our life" with all of our mind and all of our emotions. At least it is known, predictable and it does have some good in it. "Why go into a bigger space when this one is fine?" we say. That statement has to take us back to Faith and Trust. Without Faith in something bigger than ourselves we will never make the choice towards the unknown, towards that which hasn't happened yet, that isn't part of our experience. Once we have made the choice to live in synergy (with Faith); we have to Trust that synergy can survive in the world. Without Trust we cannot be on mission.

It stands to reason that people who experience the bliss of synergy will automatically bring it into their everyday lives. Yet that is not always the case. Having lived in a small world of energy with a big emphasis on forms of expression, one forgets that energy is the true creator. We have to experience energy as the creator to know the truth. However, to have that experience we have to Trust.

As you can see, *you* make the choices to be in synergy and to be on mission but the choice is all you do alone. Once you make the choice to live *in* the world of spirit and *from* the world of spirit, you have everyone's Love, Wisdom, and Power at your disposal. It is like having full access to the Federal Reserve Bank. Of course, you could choose to keep using your piggy bank, but once you are aware of the choice there really isn't one.

## *Exercises*

1. Why is mission necessary?

_____

_____

_____

_____

_____

_____

2. How does it work?

_____

_____

_____

_____

_____

_____

_____

_____

3. Why can't we have either synergy or mission by themselves?

_____

_____

_____

_____

_____

_____

_____

_____

_____

_____

_____

_____

_____

_____

_____

_____

_____

_____

_____

4. What does it mean to have the energy of all sacred females as yours?

_____

_____

_____

_____

_____

_____

_____

5. What does it mean to have the energy of all sacred males as yours?

_____

_____

_____

_____

_____

_____

_____

_____

CR

*Mission is almost*

*synonymous with*

*synergy because once*

*you are in synergy,*

*that synergy will need*

*to express.*

BO

## ♥ *Your Mission*

> *Your mission must be in alignment with the over-all goal of God's plan to bring healing to our planet.*

This includes the angels, masters and all those that work with and for this planet. You don't need a special job to be on mission. You don't need to play an instrumental solo. You just need to be able to play in the orchestra, i.e., work with one of the seven universal synergy missions. Hold the desire to express the sacred male in the way you feel you should, and you are on mission. It is that easy. You don't have to do big things just because you are now a big energy. You can do little things and get big results. Remember it is the energy that is the powerhouse not the form. I knew a lady who cleaned houses for a living who was very much on mission. She literally left golden Love energy on everything she touched. She was a carrier of synergy from the higher planes of vibration to the denser vibration of earthly forms. She was an instrument in the universal orchestra. She was on mission.

The seven synergy missions correspond to the seven chakras. Your mission may mean working with your strongest chakra or it may mean working with a weak one in order to strengthen it.

Let's take a look and see which chakra is your mission chakra. See if you feel a special pull or resonance toward any of these as you read them.

1. The mission of facilitating real expression in the world may mean you are a confronter of empty forms or it may mean you are a good hand holder for little spiritual children taking their first steps in physical expression. This is the physical (root) chakra.

2. The mission of living consciously in the world requires

helping people to deal with and own their emotions so they can get to their real truths. People on this mission may use the forms of counseling, teaching, massage, etc. This is the emotional chakra.

3. The mission of illuminating the Truth means you are willing to hold a mirror up for everyone to see all that is good in the world. You are for all that is real life. You will probably need a support group to help you keep your mind focused on positives, without hiding your head in the sand concerning the negatives. This is the mental chakra.

4. The mission of giving Birth to the God within basically means you are a spiritual midwife. You will no doubt benefit from sharing and growing with other "midwives" because spiritual midwives must live from their hearts to hold these baby heart qualities for those who are giving them birth. This is the heart chakra.

5. The mission of divine Transformation includes those who are willing to speak up for wrongs that need to be righted, or for structures of society that need to be healed. This is the throat chakra.

6. The mission of bringing Creativity to the world opens the world to more possibilities, i.e., to a bigger space. Your own creative expression can do that or you may be a supporter of others creative expression. This is the psychic chakra.

7. The mission of bringing Inspiration into the world could be anything from a beautiful smile to the writing of poetry. It could be cleaning someone's house and leaving beautiful golden Love energy behind. This is the crown chakra.

Each of these missions can take many forms. Find one that works for you. If you would benefit from some sort of support system then make sure that it is in place. You don't have to be perfect to be on mission, you just have to make two permanent choices. One is to live in the world of spirit, to be in synergy. The other is to express that energy in the world, to be on mission. Having made those two choices, you are powerful. Here is one little reminder; the heart qualities of Faith and Trust will be the keys to open the door to the world of universal synergy.

Remember, every day you have a choice. You can choose to be in synergy and be powerful, or you can stand by yourself and not be as powerful. That choice determines how well your needs get met, whether your relationships are about flow or ownership, and how much exchange happens in your giving and receiving.

CR

*The heart qualities of*

*Faith and Trust*

*are the keys to*

*open the door*

*to the world of*

*universal synergy.*

BO

## *Exercises*

1. Which chakra are you now doing mission from?

_____

_____

_____

2. What are other possible forms for expressing it?

_____

_____

_____

_____

_____

_____

_____

_____

_____

_____

_____

_____

_____

_____

_____

3. What kind of support works best for you?

_____

_____

_____

_____

_____

_____

4. How can you be more powerful in your mission?

_____

_____

_____

_____

_____

_____

_____

_____

_____

_____

## *Group Discussion*

1. Any realness is a doorway to the bigger world of spirit. Even if the other person in your interaction chooses to be unreal by not listening to their heart, you may still step in to the bigger world of spirit without them. This can be tricky because they may pull you into their non-heart subject. How do you stay heart centered?

*If the other person is in judgment, do you go there?*

*If they are in a petty, small physical place, do you go there?*

*If they are in emotional reaction, do you go there?*

2. If you play follow the leader it is because you have never been trained to hold focus. To hold a heart focus you must adjust your lens by attending to your mental, emotional, and physical bodies.

*What does that mean?*

_____

_____

_____

_____

_____

_____

_____

_____

_____

_____

_____

_____

_____

_____

_____

_____

3. When your focus takes you into the world of synergy, your vision is no longer limited to the single event that is happening at that moment. Your attention is not trapped by the current drama in your life. Your emotions can serve you in a supporting role instead of telling you continually (by their upset) that you are not in your truth.

*How do you see/feel all those who are also looking inside? What are some of the clues that tell you that you are there? What pulls you out of that space?*

_____

_____

_____

_____

_____

_____

_____

_____

_____

_____

_____

_____

_____

_____

_____

*How do you connect with people who are focused on what is real - those who are following their heart? How do you go through the doorway into the bigger world of spirit together?*

_____

_____

_____

_____

_____

*What single person or event pulls you off focus the most?*

_____

_____

*Why are they more important than you?*

_____

_____

_____

_____

_____

_____

_____

_____

4. Faith in a Power beyond your own little space is what reprograms your mental, emotional, and physical bodies. Try these two exercises:

*Remember a time when you felt judged by someone. Instead of saying that that person was being mean to you, say they were "out of focus".*

*During that experience did you feel drawn into their judgment and did you defend yourself? Instead of feeling afraid that you will be punished if you don't focus in their small space, feel powerful in your bigger connection.*

5. Your mission will be a priority only when you move from your small space to a synergy space where limitations, troubles, and fears become opportunities to resonate with everyone else who truly believes in the Power of spirit.

*What are your present opportunities?*

_____

_____

_____

_____

_____

_____

_____

_____

_____

_____

_____

_____

_____

_____

_____

_____

6. Synergy is Power and Power must express to be empowered. Thus mission, or expression, automatically follows synergy. Trust is the carrier of your powerful mission energy.

*Discuss your mission expressions.*

_____

_____

_____

_____

_____

_____

_____

_____

_____

_____

_____

_____

_____

_____

_____

_____

_____

7. Remember, if you are not in synergy you are alone.

ALONE you are always worried about whether or not you can get someone to meet your needs. In SYNERGY your needs are being met by the whole.

ALONE you either pull people into your space or push them out. You either claim them as yours or reject them. In SYNERGY relationships are about flow rather than about ownership.

ALONE, listening or sharing ends up being about giving or taking. In SYNERGY listening and sharing are for the purpose of energy exchange rather than to glean information or be validated.

*What does being in your small non-powerful space look and feel like? - As opposed to a powerful, synergy space?*

_____

_____

_____

_____

_____

_____

_____

_____

8. Are you powerful? How is that so? Are there degrees of power? Are there areas of power? Or are there just moments of power? Tell of one powerful expression.

_____

_____

_____

_____

_____

_____

_____

_____

_____

_____

_____

_____

_____

_____

_____

_____

_____

_____

CR

*The full scope of*

*synergy goes as far*

*as you are willing*

*to let your heart go.*

&

# 2

# The Four Levels of Awareness

If synergy and mission are goals, and to get there you have to resonate with all hearts, then how can you guarantee that resonating will happen? It happens when you journey to the fourth level of awareness, which is Balance. Resonating with life is about being in Balance.

You must go through the first three levels of awareness to reach the fourth level of Balance. You can get stuck at any level. A level may involve several lessons or be relatively easy depending on where you are in your growth path. You may even find yourself jumping back and forth from one level to another, sort of caught between worlds. So what are these levels?

The first level is one of self-absorption. It is the stage in your life when you have to learn about you. This requires focusing all your energy inward. Hopefully this is a time when you are gaining Power as a creator rather than a victim. This should be a time when you are learning you can

**45**

create your needs being met. At this level you are preparing to interact with the world. Here you must discover that you are Power.

The second level is the awareness of a world beyond your own. To be at this level you must come to accept your uniqueness as well as others' uniqueness. It is here that you learn the lessons of Love and Equality. This is a stage of separate but equal. You now begin to yearn for exchange of energy with others. At level two you must come to know that you are Love. Knowing this will automatically take you to the next level – that of choosing to share with others.

This third level of sharing usually requires a lot of trial and error to get it right. You may go overboard at first and give yourself away. It is, however, in giving too much that you begin to understand the need for Balance. Here, at level three, you must go through all the lessons of Wisdom, such as understanding what is about you and what is about them. Wisdom also teaches discernment about what is real and thus exchangeable. When you learn there is choice in your exchange; then you are ready for the fourth level, that of Balance.

It is here at this final stage that you become Power, Love, and Wisdom. With these three energies that you've gathered from levels one through three, you can now interact in the world as a balanced God-Being. You are no longer a taker or a giver but a Be-er. At this stage in your evolution, oneness is no longer just a goal, it is a way of life.

### ♥ *Level One – From Self-absorption to Power*

Singular focus on self is cute as a small child but it tends to become less attractive and even is called the bad name of "taker" when you fail to move beyond this level as an adult.

However, giving up manipulation and control to be safe and get your needs met can be pretty scary. Being at level one is nothing to deny or be ashamed of, but you must acknowledge where you are and that you use control and manipulation as pseudo-Power or you'll never give up those patterns in order to express real Power.

To move from self absorption to real Power you focus inward to find energies of the heart, (heart qualities), that can make you think, feel, and do differently than you have before. These heart qualities are found deep inside, way beyond the obvious awareness of an outside need. If you stop at the obvious outside need, you are powerless to meet your needs. An outside need is not a part of you so it is outside of your realm of Power. However, if you keep going inside past the obvious outside need to see what energy or heart quality it represents, then the need is part of you and you have the Power to meet it. The need has become a heart quality.

> *There is a permanent reservoir of heart energies available to each of us upon our asking so there is no excuse not to be powerful.*

Yet many of us still walk around focused on our outside needs - self absorbed and only able to take "Power" from others. Our outside needs demand all of our attention. We are stuck with seemingly no way out because we haven't yet found the inside door.

Let's take a look at some of these level one "taker" patterns:

1. Takers feel powerless to meet their own needs so they either assume the victim role or the manipulator role.
2. Since they have not yet claimed Power, their problems are always pressing.

3. They get angry when they are not given what they want because they feel a dependency on others to create for them.

4. They have to relate your situation to their own before they can understand. It is hard for them to just listen.

5. They are not automatically aware that others have needs, they have to be told. Even if they are aware, they have no time for anyone or anything that doesn't relate to them.

We get stuck in level one patterns not because we are selfish or immature but because we have not claimed our true Power. If our parents helped us to claim this Power when we were little, then this level is easy. However, if they didn't support us in claiming who we were beyond outside needs, then we may very well still be stuck (at least sometimes) in level one.

Let's do some exercises to see where you are with these level one lessons, and hopefully move closer to graduation, if that is needed.

## *Exercises*

1. From the page of heart qualities at the end of the book, write down all that support Power.

_____

_____

_____

_____

_____

_____

_____

2. In what recent situations have you acted from level one taker patterns?

_____

_____

_____

_____

_____

_____

_____

_____

3. In what recent situations have you acted from Power?

_____

_____

_____

_____

_____

4. What steps would you suggest to a recovering taker?

_____

_____

_____

_____

_____

_____

_____

_____

_____

_____

_____

_____

## ♥ *Level Two – From Separation to Love*

This can be a lonely time. You are now aware of yourself and that others exist but you haven't learned much about others yet. This is usually thought of as the awkward teen stage. Here you have gotten in touch with parts of you that you want to express; but how you expressed them at home with the folks and how you relate to each unique individual in the world are two different things. If you are forced into socialization before you claim your Power in level one then your negative patterns get reinforced even more. This happens to a lot of people. But if you have come to understand that all needs are energy needs, and that you have everything inside of you to meet those needs, then level two becomes an exciting exploration.

Let's take a look at some level two "separation" patterns:

1. Separated people have not claimed Love so they see differences in people as bad and even threatening.
2. Separation causes Love to be something done rather than something shared.
3. Separation creates a craving for someone to Love, because the separate person hasn't yet discovered the Love inside.
4. Separate people hide behind ego personalities. It doesn't matter if these personalities are weak or strong as long as they provide a shield from others' hearts.

Without Love, each person the separate person has contact with becomes an ally or enemy; not just a soul learning their lessons.

After finding your space, it is now, at level two, that you can expand your awareness to others. It is a time to celebrate differences. You can discover how the unique but different pieces of people all fit together to make up our world. At this level you enter into the world even if you don't quite know how the pieces fit. The possibilities can be exciting -- that is if you are ready for level two. If not, confusion, even depression can weigh you down because you fear being overcome by the unknown world.

You fear being overcome because you don't have a space to fit into the whole. If you are unprepared for level two, then each relationship is about conquer or be conquered, i.e., meet their need or get them to meet mine. The other option is to use the "stand off" method which is based on the belief that spaces can't fit together. It is the belief that each man is an island of individual outside needs. You struggle along in solitude. Both these methods reinforce your fears rather than teach you the lessons of Love.

So how do you learn the lessons of Love at level two? The heart qualities of Acceptance, Equality and Forgiveness, are good prep teachers. When you finally see the people in your world as struggling souls all trying to make it to level four, you bring a little more Compassion to your process. Finally you can hold them in Love.

When you become Acceptance, you are able to allow others to be at their growth level. It is then that you can become Equality and see all of us as no more than a bunch of heart qualities trying to grow. At this stage of your growth, Forgiveness becomes a natural next step. How can you not forgive when you see we are all in this learning thing together?

> *It is now clear that we are heart qualities resonating together, not a bunch of individual needs.*

As stated earlier, you may have pieces from each level. You may jump from one level to another or just jump from negative to positive on the same level. So be patient with yourself - love yourself.

*All needs are*

*energy needs*

*and you have*

*everything inside*

*of you*

*to meet those needs.*

## *Exercises*

1. What were your successes and failures as a teen in trying to fit into a bigger world?

_____

_____

_____

_____

_____

_____

_____

_____

_____

_____

_____

_____

_____

_____

_____

_____

2. How would you support a teenager in becoming a social being?

_____

_____

_____

_____

_____

_____

_____

_____

_____

_____

_____

_____

_____

_____

_____

_____

_____

_____

3. Explain what "separate but equal Love" means in relationships.

_____

_____

_____

_____

_____

_____

_____

_____

_____

_____

_____

_____

_____

_____

_____

_____

_____

_____

4. How do you know when level two is in place so you can move to level three?

_____

_____

_____

_____

_____

_____

_____

_____

_____

_____

_____

_____

_____

_____

_____

_____

_____

## ♥ *Level Three – From Caretaking to Wisdom*

Level three is a time of reaching out. You now know who you are as an energy being. Your needs outside of your heart no longer define you nor do others' outside needs define them. You understand that the real essence of a person is hiding behind their assumed needs. The real essence in the real need. Relating takes on a new meaning.

> *You do not have to waste your time and energy on anything or anyone that isn't expressing from a real energy.*

Life is abundant and full. You are now wise. You see clearly that you can only reach out to others through your own, true self-expression. You see and feel the flow. The dumping of negative energy into each others' spaces has stopped. The need to isolate yourself, in order to find a reprieve, is not pertinent. Wisdom to know what is real is much bigger than just understanding mentally what is happening. Wisdom is from and about the heart, not the mind. If you have a good understanding of who you are and how you are part of our bigger world, then you can reach out to others through your self-expression.

However, if you didn't have healthy support in order to learn Power and Love in the first two levels, then you may tend to become a "giver" (caretaker) when you are forced into level three prematurely. You are a giver when you put your energy outside of your space to meet what others' believe to be their needs. You haven't yet learned equal flow. You are just as out of balance as the taker.

Here is a checklist to see if you have reached level three in the unhealthy role of giver rather than one who shares yourself with others:

1. Givers relate their situation to yours to help you

understand.

2. They rarely ask for anything.
3. Others' problems are always more pressing than theirs.
4. They feel powerless to get support in meeting their needs.
5. They feel stronger and more competent than those to whom they are giving.
6. The outside need takes away their choice.

When you have learned self Love and Love for others, plus the real Power of seeing your own needs as energies and meeting your own needs, then level three is a time of expressing all your many parts. You don't have to give yourself away, just express. It is in mastering this level that you gain Wisdom. The Wisdom to know what is real and what is not. Only real feelings, real truths, real hugs, real gratitude, are exchangeable. They are exchangeable because they can be received; and in giving them you create a magnetic space to receive back. Giving and receiving become simultaneous. Heart energy flows through our expression and resonates with others' expression.

You also gain the Wisdom to know you have choices. Choices about what you express and the forms you express through. But again I remind you, this is only able to happen when you have matured through the first two levels.

When you get to level three you can experience great fulfillment in sharing yourself with the world. The other option is the rather dreary one of feeling stressed and empty. Feeling empty then makes the giver in you give more in an attempt to make the emptiness go away. You go into denial that you even have a space. Of course this only makes you feel even more empty so you give yourself away more. Thus, a vicious cycle starts and the possibility of reaching level four quickly vanishes.

## *Exercises*

1. How can you tell the difference between giving and sharing?

_____

_____

_____

_____

_____

_____

_____

_____

_____

_____

_____

_____

_____

_____

_____

_____

_____

_____

2. Write down one situation where you played the giver role for each of the six checklist illustrations.

_____

_____

_____

_____

_____

_____

_____

_____

_____

_____

_____

_____

_____

_____

_____

_____

_____

_____

_____

3. How could each of those six have been changed to real expression or the choice of no expression?

_____

_____

_____

_____

_____

_____

_____

_____

_____

_____

_____

_____

_____

_____

_____

_____

_____

_____

4. What happens that draws you into focusing on outside needs? Is it a habit-- when did it start? Is it a fear--of what?

_____

_____

_____

_____

_____

_____

_____

5. What is your first clue that you have emptied yourself once again?

_____

_____

_____

_____

_____

_____

_____

_____

6. How are you planning to claim Wisdom in your life?

_____

_____

_____

_____

_____

_____

_____

_____

_____

_____

_____

_____

_____

_____

_____

_____

_____

_____

7. Pick one situation in your life where you do not have fulfillment. How can you interject real expression?

_____

_____

_____

_____

_____

_____

_____

8. Pick one person you give up choice of forms with. How are you going to change that?

_____

_____

_____

_____

_____

_____

_____

_____

## ♥  *Level Four – From Childhood to Balance*

You are now ready for Balance. If you have learned who you are and that you are powerful in your space, then you can finally experience the world around you as a friendly place. This gives you permission to share the real energy and expressions of you and receive back the real energy and expression of others. Thus, a balanced flow of energy is established. It is in this flow that you feel one with all of life. You are truly alive. It is this flow that meets your needs. Since all of life is energy, you can have exchange with every living thing. You can let go of your attachment to have certain people or things meet your needs.

Here are some examples of "childhood" patterns that you may be holding on to:

1. One childhood pattern is to react to others' reactions.
2. If you feel dependent on another person to get your needs met, you are in a child role.
3. You haven't reached balanced adulthood if you still see your life as a series of performances that can bring approval or rejection.
4. Children see their small world as special. Balanced people see all life as sacred.
5. Feeling you must act grown up in all areas keeps you in denial about the size of your heart qualities and out of Balance.

*Balance is about a continuous flow of energy.*

It is about giving and receiving becoming one thing. It is about being a part of the life force of the universe. It is your birthright, but you have to grow each piece one at a time to be in balance. Parts of you may be grown and other parts may still be young or not even born. You may be fully adult in the heart energy of Honesty, but only a child in Spontaneity. Perhaps Adventure hasn't even been born in you yet. This doesn't mean you are less than anybody else, it simply means you have your own growth pattern.

To summarize, you must move from self-absorption to self-awareness in level one. In level two you must be aware of yourself and equally aware of others. In level three, self-expression becomes the mode of sharing rather than caretaking. In level four you get to experience Balance where you can resonate with life.

*Balance is the doorway to synergy.*

## *Exercises*

1. What are the three levels that lead to Balance?

_____

_____

_____

_____

2. How can you experience Balance without being totally mature in each level? Give examples.

_____

_____

_____

_____

_____

_____

_____

_____

_____

_____

_____

_____

_____

3. How can you know when there is a return of energy? For example, when are you in Balance? What does it feel like?

_____

_____

_____

_____

_____

_____

_____

_____

_____

_____

_____

_____

_____

_____

_____

_____

_____

4. What is your biggest resistance to Balance? What are you going to do about it?

_____

_____

_____

_____

_____

_____

_____

_____

_____

_____

_____

_____

_____

_____

_____

_____

_____

_____

_____

CR

*Balance
is the doorway
to Synergy.*

&

## *Group Discussion*

1. At what level of awareness would you classify yourself in each of the heart qualities listed at the end of the book?

*Write the level (1-4) next to each heart quality.*

2. Every single situation, conversation and dream gives you a clue about who you are.

*What is your process of looking inward? Do you leave any of those out? Which ones and why?*

---

---

---

---

---

---

---

---

---

---

---

---

---

---

---

3. Defining yourself by your heart qualities will change your perception of tasks.

*Do you evaluate yourself by focusing on how well or poorly you handled something or by seeing what energy you were expressing?*

_____

_____

_____

_____

_____

_____

_____

_____

_____

_____

_____

_____

_____

4. You may take care of everyone's needs so you can stay busy and not look inward.

*Do you have a first line of defense so you won't have to go inward? Think of situations where this happened.*

_____

_____

_____

_____

_____

_____

_____

_____

_____

_____

_____

_____

_____

_____

_____

_____

_____

5. Your inward journey can take you to a real space or you may find yourself acting out a role that is all too familiar.

*Do your inward journeys take you to a real space, i.e., a heart quality? Or do they take you to a role, such as caretaker, victim, unworthy person, etc.*

_____

_____

_____

_____

_____

_____

_____

_____

_____

_____

_____

_____

_____

_____

6. Look at a conversation you had recently. Did you find yourself acting out your favorite role?

*What was your response? Where did you end up in your inward journey?*

_____

_____

_____

_____

_____

_____

_____

_____

_____

_____

_____

_____

_____

_____

_____

_____

7. Your awareness has to go beyond your immediate focus to include everything that is happening on all levels – physical, emotional, mental, and spiritual.

*What is your present awareness quotient? Does your awareness leave you out? Are you aware of only what goes on around you? Or does it only include you?*

_____

_____

_____

_____

_____

_____

_____

_____

_____

_____

_____

_____

_____

_____

_____

_____

8. Obsession is the opposite of awareness in that your awareness gets stuck on one subject.

*Do you spend most of your day obsessing about what you need to do, what has happened to you, or about what you want?*

_____

_____

_____

_____

_____

_____

_____

_____

_____

_____

_____

_____

_____

_____

_____

_____

9. You shouldn't have to go on vacations if there is flow in all of your life because with flow renewal is constant.

*Is your life ordered this way? What are your priorities?*

_____

_____

_____

_____

_____

_____

_____

_____

_____

_____

_____

_____

_____

_____

_____

_____

10. For example, obligation (the name) is an outside pressure that pushes against you while you are trying to express, with an end result of exhaustion.

*Can you give your outside pressures names? Try to describe the personality of each. What is the end result of each?*

_____

_____

_____

_____

_____

_____

_____

_____

_____

_____

_____

_____

_____

_____

_____

_____

11. To identify your blocks to self-expression ask yourself:

*"Are my expressions motivated by me or by the outside?"* List both.

_____

_____

_____

_____

_____

_____

_____

_____

_____

_____

_____

_____

_____

_____

_____

_____

_____

_____

12. For every unbalanced relationship you have in your life there is a piece of you unclaimed.

*Talk about one of your unbalanced relationships and look at your unclaimed expression.*

_____

_____

_____

_____

_____

_____

_____

_____

_____

_____

_____

_____

_____

_____

_____

_____

_____

_____

_____

13. For every piece claimed and expressed there is an equal amount of real energy coming back to you.

*What real energies are you receiving? How are they coming to you?*

_____

_____

_____

_____

_____

_____

_____

_____

_____

_____

_____

_____

_____

_____

_____

_____

_____

_____

14. You are part of the whole. You no longer have to make things happen. People and things flow to you. They are already part of your world you just have to be receptive.

*Is it easier to see people who flow into your life as part of you, or things that flow into your life as part of you? List both and after each say "this is part of me, it is part of flow".*

_____

_____

_____

_____

_____

_____

_____

_____

_____

_____

_____

_____

_____

_____

_____

Let go of what you think you should be receiving and just receive what is there. Once your real expression hits the air waves you are in flow. That is all there is to it. The problem is we try to receive the form rather than the energy, or we try to make the energy bigger than it is. Just receive what is, with gratitude, and it (you) will grow.

# 3

# Further Along
# the Road to Balance

In the last chapter on the four levels of awareness you dug deep inside to discover who you are. You found that who you are is separate from what you do. The real pieces you have discovered must be honored by letting them have a space of their own to "incubate". When they have grown up enough to have a voice, you must let them express. You discovered that the energy you send out is immediately returned; all you have to do is receive it. It is in this giving and receiving flow that Balance is found.

Frustration often comes when you try to integrate your newfound parts into the world. This chapter on Balance will help you become part of the bigger world. You will jump from being small Power, Love and Wisdom to being big Power, Love and Wisdom. You are on the road to synergy – the ultimate spiritual journey.

We will again focus on the four levels of awareness

leading to Balance. First, you will see how the heart qualities you claim can become tools of Power in building your world. Next, you will see that all your separate spaces belong together. You will then see how everyone's expression benefits everybody else. And finally you will, at the very least, glimpse the magnitude of Power that is yours when you claim your place as part of the whole.

## ♥ *Power*

As you recall from the last chapter, the first level of awareness is about finding the real parts of you. These are precious gifts that you have to offer others and the world. These are the parts of you that make you unique and special. But you may get lost in comparing forms rather than appreciating the energy, which is the true gift. You look at your face and say that is your identity. You compare your body to others and give yourself a grade. You truly believe those forms make you attractive to others. You attach to the belief that doing something well enhances your worth. You have so identified yourself with the forms of your doing and having that you have forgotten who you really are. You are the energy behind those forms. It is the energy that is the Power. It is the energy that attracts. It is the energy that makes things happen.

You may hear the truth that it is the energy that makes things happen and then try to manipulate this profound truth. You may use it as an excuse not to do anything. This doesn't work because doing brings the energy into the physical. Thus, doing is very important, but it is not the source of Power. Spiritual manipulation also happens when you want to come from the heart but you don't trust the heart to lead so you try to fill obligations with heart energy.

Stuffing your real self into forms that don't fit is like wearing hand-me-downs that are too small.

When you meditate, you get in touch with different heart qualities, but you have a hard time making the jump to identify yourself as those heart qualities in the everyday world. You profess to believe you are more than what you do and say, but your reality belies that belief.

> *Your world will hold Power only when you begin to "live from the inside out".*

When you get it that you are energy and energy holds Power, nothing can limit you ever again. Your life will be about who you are, not about what you do. You will realize that within each of us we speak a universal language of the heart. It is in speaking that language that the world responds. Maybe not each and every person, but those that are real in the universe respond. You don't even have to go looking for those that are real. All you have to do is put out real energy and it will come back to you.

CR

*The real parts*

*of you*

*are the precious gifts*

*that you have*

*to offer others*

*and the world.*

BD

## *Exercises*

1. Give examples from your life when you experienced the truth that Energy Makes Things Happen!

_____

_____

_____

_____

_____

_____

_____

_____

_____

_____

_____

_____

_____

_____

_____

_____

_____

2. Do you ever try to manipulate spiritual energy? How?

_____

_____

_____

_____

_____

_____

_____

_____

3. What forms do you have in your life right now that limit your Power? (Clue: they are empty forms.)

_____

_____

_____

_____

_____

_____

_____

_____

4. Is your Power pulled away by the following forms, or is it securely within you?

    a.) Losing or leaving your job.

    b.) Moving from your home.

    c.) Visiting with your family.

    d.) The death of someone very close to you.

_____

_____

_____

_____

_____

_____

_____

_____

_____

_____

_____

_____

_____

_____

_____

ॐ

*Every heart quality*

*has many tones,*

*together*

*they make a*

*symphony.*

ॐ

♥ *Love*

Your gifts have now been found and recognized, and in their expression you have found Power. You are now able to see how everybody's piece helps to make up the whole. My gift compliments your gift and vice versa. You made it past comparing forms in level one so you can now see that your piece of real and mine are different; but at the same time they are equal. They are only parts of a bigger picture.

We need each other because we can become more together than we can become individually. I am not talking about meeting each other's needs. We are each complete within ourselves and can certainly meet our own needs. Yet, each complete unit must find its place among the other units to be all that it can be. Every piece of the puzzle fits with the other pieces to make a picture. Every heart quality has many tones; together they make a symphony. It is at this level that we learn how to really Love.

Isn't Love that "thing" you have wanted since day one? You have longed to be accepted for who you are. You have ached to be seen and heard all the way to your real core. You have come up with all kinds of schemes and plans to get Love, but usually all you end up with is someone kindly looking on or giving you an understanding pat on the shoulder. The truth of the matter is, you can't get there by viewing each other as separate. You can only get there when you join together with others.

> *Love is an energy of exchange, a resonating together - not a package you hand to someone.*

We have worked so hard to find ourselves, to define and protect our space, that we are terrified of disappearing again. We are under the false impression that we will be swallowed up if we resonate with someone else.

The real truth is, you will finally find yourself when you become part of a whole. An arm or a leg by itself does very little good, but when they are part of a whole body they are valuable.

Do you live in constant fear that your needs won't be met? If so, it's because you don't know how to meet them yourself. However, if each individual need you have is an energy need and not a form, then a group doesn't hinder you from expressing that energy. In fact, your expression will be enhanced by the group, if there is a synergy present. When this happens, your needs become Power tools, not heavy demanding weights around your neck.

Once you understand that your needs are simply heart energies that connect you to other hearts, life becomes an experience of Love. Life defined as Love is so much easier than life defined as struggle. But, until life and Love become synonymous, struggle it will be. If you are not freely giving and receiving your energy needs from the heart, then you must be constantly bartering for those needs.

## *Exercises*

1. Pick two groups you are a part of, (like family, work, etc.) and see if you allow yourself to be part of the whole. How or why not?

_____

_____

_____

_____

_____

_____

_____

_____

_____

_____

_____

_____

_____

_____

_____

_____

_____

2. How can you be part of a whole and not feel you are losing your needs? If you get to a real inside need as opposed to a pseudo outside need, should you tell those around you what it is? Define how this can work for you.

_____

_____

_____

_____

_____

_____

_____

_____

_____

_____

_____

_____

_____

_____

_____

_____

_____

3. Define a group structure (examples: a game, work team).
   a.) What about that structure makes you comfortable or uncomfortable?
   (Number of people, pace of work, tasks, rules, language, formality.)

_____

_____

_____

_____

_____

_____

_____

_____

_____

_____

_____

_____

_____

_____

_____

_____

b.) Does your need for comfort or dealing with the discomfort keep you from being part of the whole? How?

_____

_____

_____

_____

_____

_____

_____

_____

_____

_____

_____

_____

_____

_____

_____

_____

_____

4. Write about the statement that Love can only happen when you are part of a whole. What would that love look and feel like? Is it difficult to come by?

_____

_____

_____

_____

_____

_____

_____

_____

_____

_____

_____

_____

_____

_____

_____

_____

_____

CR

*You will finally*

*find yourself*

*when you become*

*part of*

*a whole.*

BC

♥   *Wisdom*

Wisdom is about expressing who you are in the world. This can be a danger point if you didn't get the "forms" issue completely confronted in the level one Power discussions.

> *If you judge one experience better or worse than another, then you are missing the Wisdom needed to see every experience as an opportunity to learn a new piece of who you are, and/or to empower a piece of you that you have already claimed.*

There are no bad experiences! I repeat, there are no bad experiences! So there is no reason to hold back expressing your energy, or essence, into forms. Forms are not going to go sour or backfire. They are not going to mess up your life forever. They are simply containers for your heart energies. And your heart only expresses your sacred self, your highest good.

It takes Wisdom to express yourself in the world; but not the kind of Wisdom you have trusted in all these years. It is not a Wisdom with no mistakes and no wrong answers. It is a Wisdom that greets every experience with exuberance and courage. It uses every experience as an opportunity to claim a new part or empower an already existing part of you. The "mistakes" and "wrong answers" are forms just as the "right answers" and the "right actions" are forms. Some forms pull new pieces from you and some of the forms reuse old pieces of you - both are good.

If you can now see every experience as a form or container for your energy, then you can be grateful for every single interaction with others. Remember there are no bad experiences. If you can really take this in, there will be no more judgment about the form or the interaction, only Gratitude. If you live life from this place, then everyone brings you a gift. Everyone supports your growth, and you give everyone a gift and support for his or her growth. People will be precious to you.

You may say, "What about the relationship that hurt me so badly?" "What did I get from that other than pain and grief?" "How about the time I was in a car accident?" "Surely that was a *bad* experience."

The answer to these questions is found in the awareness that the heart must be the subject, not the emotions nor the mind. Life will be viewed differently when seen through the Wisdom of the heart.

> *Wisdom knows that life is all about becoming who you were meant to be.*

## *Exercises*

1. List your present "bad experiences". What opportunities do they hold to find or empower something inside you?

_____

_____

_____

_____

_____

_____

_____

_____

_____

_____

_____

_____

_____

_____

_____

_____

_____

2. Which do you have the most resistance to: claiming a new piece of yourself or empowering an old one? Explain.

3. What decisions have you made in your life that you consider bad?

_____

_____

_____

_____

_____

_____

_____

_____

_____

_____

_____

_____

_____

_____

_____

_____

_____

_____

_____

4. For each of your answers in question #3, there is a piece of you still unclaimed from the experience. Stop and meditate to search for that piece now.

_____

_____

_____

_____

_____

_____

_____

_____

_____

_____

_____

_____

_____

_____

_____

_____

_____

_____

5. How can you use Wisdom to look at life?
(Hint: Wisdom is not about being right but seeing every experience as an opportunity.)

_____

_____

_____

_____

_____

_____

_____

_____

_____

_____

_____

_____

_____

_____

_____

_____

CR

*Wisdom uses every*

*experience as an*

*opportunity to claim*

*a new part or*

*empower an already*

*existing part of you.*

EC

## ♥ *Balance*

If Balance only happens when the exchange of gifts, or energies, takes place, then you can only receive what you make a space for. If you ask someone to do for you and you don't give a heart quality in the asking, then there is no space to receive back. Of course the reverse is also true. If someone asks of you and gives only a form, then you do not have a space to give to them and they get nothing.

This all sounds a little like you are at the mercy of others to be open to give and to receive. After working hard to give up the victim role you certainly aren't eager to go back to being at the mercy of the world. Let me assure you this is not the case.

> *Your gift, no matter what size or shape, is a magnetic energy.*

Each heart quality has the ability to literally pull real energy to it. Its range of pull is much greater than through the person standing in front of you. So if the person in front of you is not receptive, then your magnetic gift goes out and touches where there is a receptor. That receptor vibrates, or resonates, and the flow comes back to be received by you. It is when you reach this stage of magnetic flow, that you find real Balance in life.

Unfortunately you may have been confused about Balance because you have seen yourself as separate. When you perceive each person's space as separate rather than connected, then you believe you must give something to him or her - and in turn they must give you something back. In this mode, giving and receiving are separate acts. However, when you are in Balance in the world, (when you have become part of the whole), then giving and receiving happen simultaneously. A flow is set up that empowers both of the people that are giving and receiving.

> *The more people you resonate with the more powerful you are.*

Are you scared when asked to be part of a bigger mission or goal because you are afraid of feeling that much Power? Do you just ride along and leech off the group to feel safe or do you take charge of the group to feel safe? It is time to claim that your space is as powerful as the sum of the parts. It is only in stepping beyond your fears, and giving the gift of you to the world, that you receive more than your gift.

To be all that you came to be, your individual spirit has to reconnect with the universal spirit. Down here on earth universal spirit lives in physical bodies. Because you are so used to separate spaces, you feel that to reconnect you have to make it happen. In reality the Power you gain from being part of a synergy group works *for* you to create flow in your life.

It is hard for some of us to turn loose of feeling responsible for the whole. On the other hand, it is just as hard for some to not leech off the whole because we claim no responsibility for our individual space. When the "responsible" ones and the "leeches" get together, we develop imbalance. The ideal is a situation where complete individual units connect with each other to make a whole. When this happens, the sum is greater than the parts and Balance is the theme.

So you say, "but where do groups exist that have individuals responsible for their own spaces, i.e., their own feelings, thoughts, actions, and heart qualities?" There really aren't any. But if, for example, the intent of the group is about Truth; then Truth will be pulled from each member of the group. You don't have to choose to baby-sit the weak or be pulled in by the control freaks. Insecurity and control are just patterns developed out of fear. The heart energy of Truth does exist in these people, (as does all heart energies) even though they haven't let go of their fear patterns. If their Truth gets pulled forward by your magnetic gift of Truth, then they can choose to define that they wish Truth to happen. At that point, fear lost its power and Balance was allowed in.

The heart energy defined will be there. You can choose to participate only with that energy. You do not have to participate with their fear patterns. Get what you came for! As you can see, you don't have to find perfect people, just make sure the intent of the group is pure and you will go home with more than you brought.

Being part of something bigger than just you requires individual preparation first and then Courage to jump from small Power, Love and Wisdom to big Power, Love and Wisdom. You may want it but you are afraid of it. For example, my personal favorite mission is the Adawehi Healing Center. Adawehi is a mission group established with the goal of bringing healing energy to the planet. It is a group where the sum is greater than the parts. But it is not about people giving up themselves in self-sacrifice. It is a place where each part is the Power of the sum. It is a group where a gift given by one individual becomes as powerful as the whole. A group where a gift received by one individual empowers the whole. Remember, it is not about perfect people but perfect intent that joins you in synergy, and gives each person a gift. By being part of a group that chooses to include the heart, you can take your next growth step towards becoming more Power, Love, and Wisdom.

If you accept that you are energy and your energy space is part of a bigger space, you will become more powerful than you can ever imagine. All you have to do is claim responsibility for your individual space so that it has existence, by choosing the heart, and let it join with all the other "real spaces" in the universe to become part of the whole, a part of synergy. We can heal the planet with this plan.

## *Exercises*

1. How do you block Support, sometimes even when you have asked for it?

_____

_____

_____

_____

_____

_____

_____

_____

_____

_____

_____

_____

_____

_____

2. How does a request directed to one person, end up coming to you from another source?

_____

_____

_____

_____

_____

_____

_____

_____

_____

_____

_____

_____

_____

_____

_____

_____

_____

_____

3. What is the difference between you in your separate space and you as part of a whole? Give examples.

_____

_____

_____

_____

_____

_____

_____

_____

_____

_____

_____

_____

_____

_____

_____

_____

_____

_____

_____

_____

4. How far can your vision go? Is the idea of healing the planet too big for your mind to comprehend? Write out your vision.

_____

_____

_____

_____

_____

_____

_____

_____

_____

_____

_____

_____

_____

_____

_____

_____

*Group Discussion*

1. Being honest about what your gifts are, content and size is not easy, but keep in mind a mastered form doesn't always mean a big gift.

*Ask the group who you are and who you are not. Write down the responses to contemplate later.*

_____

_____

_____

_____

_____

_____

_____

_____

_____

_____

_____

_____

_____

_____

_____

2. Maybe the biggest block to being honest about who you are is your embarrassment about who you aren't. That part of you has usually received criticism at some time or another in a way that was emotionally and sometimes even physically hurtful.

*Where are your embarrassed areas? Why do you feel you should fill those spaces? Write your answers then share with the group.*

_____

_____

_____

_____

_____

_____

_____

_____

_____

_____

_____

_____

_____

_____

_____

3. Sharing yourself is about feeling free to "come out" to others. This doesn't mean that others have to interact with all the parts of you, but you can't hide pieces if you honor your whole self. As strange as it may seem, you may often hide the parts of you that you value the most to keep them safe; but a child hidden in a closet can not ever become strong.

*What part of you do you need to let "come out"? You may choose to answer some of these questions before you come to the discussion group to share.*

_____

_____

_____

_____

_____

_____

_____

_____

_____

_____

_____

_____

_____

4. To be part of a whole you have to be able to listen to what energy a person is bringing, without getting tangled up in their words, emotions, thoughts, or needs. By the way, you can't get tangled up in your own either.

*Rate yourself as a listener. Be honest about the parts that get tangled up.*

_____

_____

_____

_____

_____

_____

_____

_____

_____

_____

_____

_____

_____

_____

_____

_____

5. You block the magnetic Power of the heart to pull to itself everything that it needs by being responsible for the empty spaces in others. Example:  I had a friend once that was loud and pushy to cover up her emotional vulnerability. In her presence, I would become very quiet and small to protect her scared part that was covered by her boisterous part. Then one day I stopped feeling responsible for her vulnerable part, and guess what? I started feeling Love for her and from her.

*Look at you with a friend. How do you fill in the spaces? Do you fill the space with Love?*

_____

_____

_____

_____

_____

_____

_____

_____

_____

_____

_____

_____

_____

_____

6. Commitment to the whole is not just doing things for the whole, but being a part of it.

*Discuss what keeps you from fully being part of the Universal whole. What doing do you identify as you?*
*As you become aware of your separateness, what patterns keep you there? What keeps you part of the whole?*

_____

_____

_____

_____

_____

_____

_____

_____

_____

_____

_____

_____

_____

_____

_____

_____

_____

7. As you move into being a "Universal Spiritual Person" physical groups will become more a part of your life. They will become a place to which you bring your gifts of expression to be empowered.

*Which of your gifts of expression could be empowered by a "group reception"? Which are being empowered now?*

_____

_____

_____

_____

_____

_____

_____

_____

_____

_____

_____

_____

_____

_____

_____

_____

*It is only in stepping*

*beyond your fears,*

*and giving the gift of*

*you to the world,*

*that you receive more*

*than your gift.*

# 4

# More Synergy

Once you have reached balance and have tasted the world of spirit, your life is changed. You no longer want to put a crown on the mundane things in life. You want to hold a picture of the bigger vision and let the real jewels of life shine. Synergy doesn't fit into all your old relationship patterns. It doesn't fit into your old avoidance patterns. It doesn't fit into your old get things done patterns. You can't put new wine into old wineskins. So, to now live from the world of spirit, all the old patterns have to be discarded and replaced with new ones that recognize and honor the oneness of us all.

Once you learn how to define the intent of your heart, you can then join in synergy with all the beings that hold that same heart quality so it can manifest in the world. The concept, though clear and simple, is at the same time alien. In your heart you know that you are part of the whole and should act as part of the whole. However, your ego still believes it can choose to keep you separate by choosing patterns defined out of fear instead of patterns defined by the heart.

Your heart may first choose to live your life from and with the support of synergy, but your free will may make a second choice to live from all your old patterns. As you can readily see, choice #2 just canceled out choice #1. Even if the choice to live from your old patterns is made because you don't know any new ones, it still blocks synergy. So to save you from your old patterns let's look at some new patterns you can live your life through.

## ♥  *Relationship Patterns*

To live in synergy and be in relationship you have to have patterns that help you to look at the heart of the person rather than their charm or dysfunctional behavior. If their intent is not heart based, then you must learn how to stay in your heart even when they are not. This requires a lot of intentional focus at first because you may be so used to the old pattern of *looking at behavior or words rather than the heart* that you forget they are not really the subject.

Here's an example; your neighbor, Janice, calls and asks you to help her with her three young children. She says she needs to run to town to do some grocery shopping and she just can't bear the thought of bringing along the kids this time. Now, Janice is a good friend and has helped you out before so you owe her one. Your old pattern might be to act out of obligation. After all isn't that what friends are for? Then of course, you could justify your helping out by saying you care about her well being and that you want her to have a peaceful trip to the store. The intent of your heart cannot be just any good heart energy you might have ever had in the past towards Janice.

*Your heart energy is based on what energy is being pulled from you at the moment.*

If Janice is truly asking for Support, rather than "you owe me one", then by listening to your heart you can actually feel the energy of Support resonate between you. You are then in synergy with each other. Remember, synergy is the resonating of your hearts, not "doing the good deed". However, by doing the act of baby-sitting you can allow the spiritual energy of Support to express in your physical world.

Now let's take that same example, but this time Janice is coming from the place of "you owe me". She reminds you that she recently watched your sick child for an entire day so that you wouldn't miss work. If you listen beyond the words to the energy, (which you can do if you listen from your heart), you will hear that there is something that needs clearing before you can proceed with Support. Even if you have Support in your heart, you cannot be in synergy with Janice until her "stuff" is cleared. Please don't hear that as a command to take care of her emotions. You could simply ask her to share where she is coming from to "clear the air". You have now given her the opportunity to be in synergy with you. If she is in denial about her motivation, then you can still be in synergy with all the beings that are holding the energy of Support, but not in synergy with Janice. You will then need to tell her you can't baby-sit for her right now because if you do, you will be empowering a small relationship space with her. You can explain to her that you don't want to come over out of an obligation, rather than telling her that she is just not able to receive Support.

Every time you act, you are literally defining relationship spaces, i.e., energy containers for heart qualities. If you act from a synergistic place you have made the relationship stronger. If, on the other hand, you act outside of synergy; then you are redefining the relationship to be about the unreal.

*Unreal causes your relationships to become smaller and weaker.*

Forget how you want it to be. It is in how you respond that you tell your unconscious what you believe to be truth.

Refusing to baby-sit would be the heart thing to do if synergy is not possible, but your old patterns of worry come in and say such things as: "Janice will be mad at me." "I might lose Janice as my friend and after all I don't have that many friends." "What if she tells the other neighbors?" "I must be awfully selfish." "It won't hurt to do it just this once." You can respond for your heart even if your emotions aren't in agreement.

What happens to your relationship with Janice if she stays in denial? Every time synergy is expressed in a relationship the relationship is empowered. Every time you empower separation, the relationship gets smaller. After awhile, it would feel less and less satisfying to be with Janice. If you keep the same patterns of behavior in a relationship but those patterns are empty of positive intent, then not only does the relationship get smaller but your personal space does also.

*You cannot just visit synergy and grow; you have to move in.*

Everything you say, think, feel, or do impacts your personal space. You are either connecting from the heart with your expression or you are not. If you are not you just took a vote to mark off a few points of your Power. On the other hand, if your expression connects with the heart of the universe, you have grown.

Another relationship pattern that is commonly used to cancel out synergy is the *best friend* pattern. It goes like this: "Joe" is your best friend because you like the same music and your kids both play soccer. Oh yes, your wives get along well also and you carpool to work together. This pattern allows a feeling of comfort to override what is real. Connecting from comfort may be emotionally and physically satisfying, but it is not going to empower anything spiritual. It is not synergy and it does not create synergy.

You may say, "I am in a feel good space when I am around my best friend because we've known each other so long." It is fine to be in a feel good space. Comfort in friendship is not a bad thing. Yet to have synergy with all humankind, you cannot be attached to patterns of safety and comfort to be real. You should be able to be comfortable because you are acting or speaking from your heart, not because the pattern is comfortable.

To be in a feel good space in the presence of a friend is not the same as being in synergy. The intent of both friends must be to keep a clear space for their hearts to resonate. You must be together because your hearts are together not because it is as comfortable as an old shoe.

Let me share a true story. Sarah and Barbara were close friends for fifteen years. They shared the misery of their marriages, listening intently to each other's complaints. They would spend hours each week on the telephone philosophizing about the meaning of life and how unhappy they were. They went on excursions together most Saturdays to get out of the house to laugh and play together while their husbands sat in front of the TV watching sports and old western movies. They were truly "best friends". After years of being unhappily married, Sarah finally filed for a divorce. Barbara was there for Sarah during her ugly custody and settlement battle. Not long after the divorce was final Sarah was at Barbara's home for a Fourth of July barbecue. Barbara's husband had a bit too much to drink and came on to Sarah. When Barbara found out she threw her relationship with Sarah out the window. There obviously wasn't a lot of real synergy between them to begin with or the relationship would have been bigger than the barbecue incident. What they shared all those years was merely a feel good space based upon commonality.

What was created by that relationship in those fifteen years? Both women felt powerless to change the misery in their lives.

They could mentally go into big spaces through philosophy, but emotionally they only facilitated and comforted each other's misery. In the physical, they were totally "frozen" for years. They were both loving, nurturing people but the relationship definition kept them both small and powerless. Their hearts were not in synergy. It behooves you to check out every relationship to see the motivation behind it. If it seems nice but there is no synergy, then you must throw it out. If you can't give your heart first rating, then what is life really about?

A favorite relationship pattern that is used to cancel out synergy is *my need is a form.* You get a call from a distant cousin and he asks you if he can camp on your family's land. Is this a need or a form? It is an empty form unless there is a heart's intent behind the cousin's request; and even then only the heart energy is the need. So let's say the heart energy that the cousin wishes to express through camping is Peace. You have a small problem. You have just planted crops and flowers and this cousin lacks awareness and appreciation of such things. The heart quality that you hold around your land is Beauty. Obviously there are different needs here. If both of you recognize that your need is an energy, and your cousin is not attached to the form of camping on your family's land, then reconciliation could be quite possible. You can work together to find a form for your cousin's Peace need and your Beauty need if you just remember needs are energies, not forms. Perhaps your cousin could stay in your house instead of outside, or the two of you might go camping together somewhere else. The possibilities are endless when the attachment to the form is removed.

You have now established that your personal needs are energies. Let's take it a step further to say that these need energies can create forms. For example, when your clothing purchase is backed by the energy of Comfort, you will buy clothes that you will wear a lot. However if you buy clothes for whom you *ought* to be or *hope* to be then you will never feel at home in your clothes. It is obvious from this example that you have to be with the need energy long enough to get to know it and claim it in order to express it in your life.

Let's say you have just claimed your need to be Creative. At first your energy of Creativity may be small and it will manifest in a small way, but as it grows it will find bigger and bigger forms to express through. For instance, when Thomas and Claire moved to a small town after living in the city for 25 years, they started to express their Creativity through new forms. In the city they had labeled Play and Creativity as one and the same and attached it to forms such as movies and restaurants. In the country, without many movies or restaurants to choose from, they started playing board games. While this was Play it also sparked their Creativity because they changed the game rules often. After awhile, their Creativity started defining forms that had always been vetoed in the past. Gardening, for example, had only represented an overwhelming amount of work. However, with the growing Creativity they designed and planted a garden from sheer delight because the energy of Creativity was now bigger and thus large enough to fit the form.

How does this concept work when you are in a group situation?

How can you get your needs met through agreed upon forms without manipulating the group, forging ahead and pulling them along, or withdrawing?

> *You are going to have to give up all expression patterns, from the way you think to the way you emotionally respond, if you truly want to change your relationship patterns so they work in a group.*

You may have to ask for time out to find what energy is your real need. You may have to redefine several times how you want to express yourself as an energy grows and you become a different person. It will be necessary to know the other group members' needs as energies also. They may also want time to "process". Eventually the group will be ready to decide on forms (structures or actions) that will work for everyone's good.

Let's say that four people have volunteered to conduct a fundraising event for their favorite organization. They all four have a different form in mind. Sue wants to sell candy. Jeanne thinks a dance would be more fun. Kathy loves to make handcrafted gifts and is sure others would enjoy that too. While Niki is convinced that soliciting donations from corporate America is a real possibility. What is the answer? Obviously they have started at the wrong end - the forms. If they back up and see what heart quality wants to express in each of those forms, then the attachment to the form goes away. The feelings get soothed, and their real needs get met. Sue's heart need is Simplicity, Jeanne's is Play, Kathy's is Creativity, and Niki's is Abundance. Their next step will be to find a form that allows them each an expression that will allow their heart to grow, and thus meet a need.

One possibility would be to sponsor a one-act comedy play put on by the 6th grade children form the local elementary school. Sue could resonate with the children's Simplicity. Kathy could use her Creativity in creating the costumes. Jeanne could let her own inner child come out to Play with the students. And Niki could express Abundance through the money brought in from the fundraiser. It is now the heart's need for expression that guides their behavior.

As you can see group interaction with the good of all in mind is a long way from the normal "push things through" method. This only works with conscious, conscientious people. These are not people free of fear patterns, but people who recognize the importance of defining from the heart.

Another nasty pattern is the one where we use *common language to manipulate interactions* (this can be any language two people have in common). For instance, two friends have agreed to clear all bad feelings between them. One says, "I need to clear something with you". What they really mean is, "I need you to stop doing what you're doing, and if I tell you it makes me feel bad maybe you'll stop". A person in a friendship with the definition of Honesty may say, "I feel in my heart we should sit down and talk", when what they really mean is, "I emotionally want to get you to act my way."

Then there is the relationship with the intent of Balance where one of the two says, "I am going to define our relationship smaller because you don't share as much as I share." The person is really saying this to <u>not</u> let the relationship become smaller. It is said as a manipulation to keep it the same size or make it even bigger by using guilt to get the other person to share.

> *Synergy requires us to speak the truth about who we are twenty four hours a day.*

> *It demands that our relationship definitions and our personal intents match.*

You can't hide behind language, forms, behaviors, or similarities in relationships and stay in synergy. You have to give up those old patterns of relating and listen to your heart. Your emotions as well as your mind will go crazy at first when you take away their believed securities. However, they will soon discover synergy is a much more peaceful and powerful way to live.

## *Exercises*

1. How would you handle these patterns of behavior and stay in synergy:

   a.) You need a loan of money, someone offers it, but they have issues around money.

_____

_____

_____

_____

_____

_____

_____

_____

_____

_____

_____

_____

_____

_____

_____

_____

b.) A friend floats in and out of synergy in a very unpredictable pattern.

_____

_____

_____

_____

_____

_____

_____

_____

_____

_____

_____

_____

_____

_____

_____

_____

_____

c.) Someone you aren't close to asks you how you are doing and you are not doing very well.

_____

_____

_____

_____

_____

_____

_____

_____

_____

_____

_____

_____

_____

_____

_____

_____

_____

_____

d.) Humor has been one of your fix all's.

_____

_____

_____

_____

_____

_____

_____

_____

_____

_____

_____

_____

_____

_____

_____

_____

_____

e.) Your family offers you physical support but judges how you live your life.

_____

_____

_____

_____

_____

_____

_____

_____

_____

_____

_____

_____

_____

_____

_____

_____

_____

_____

_____

2. Name three relationships and list your comfort connects. Be careful; people like to justify that these are synergy connects.

_____

_____

_____

_____

_____

_____

_____

_____

_____

_____

_____

_____

_____

_____

_____

_____

_____

_____

3. Identify the heart qualities that you now own. Name areas, (such as work, friendships, spiritual growth) not forms, where you express these. Be specific.

_____

_____

_____

_____

_____

_____

_____

_____

_____

_____

_____

_____

_____

_____

_____

_____

_____

_____

4. List all the other areas of your life not listed above. What would happen if you were to eliminate the parts of your life that do not express heart qualities? What fears come up?

_____

_____

_____

_____

_____

_____

_____

_____

_____

_____

_____

_____

_____

_____

_____

_____

_____

_____

5. Write down as many "family" sayings as come to mind. Check to see if they support the real you rather than the ego you.

_____

_____

_____

_____

_____

_____

_____

_____

_____

_____

_____

_____

_____

_____

_____

_____

_____

_____

☙

*Every time*

*you act,*

*you are literally*

*defining*

*relationship spaces.*

❧

### ♥ *Avoidance Patterns*

Living from the energy of all connected hearts, (the synergy of spirit), means you have to be honest with yourself about everything. It is more than just telling the truth about what happened.

*It is seeing anything and everything that is not in synergy as dishonest.*

If you are willing to live even a portion of your life in dishonesty then you still have avoidance patterns. So it becomes necessary to look first at what keeps you dishonest. The need to look special in order to have Love is one big lie that is perpetuated daily by the advertising media. You may even take it a step further and tell yourself that you not only need to have another's approval physically, but also you must have their mental and emotional approval if you are to be loved.

Another lie that you may be perpetuating is the belief that you are your patterns of behavior. Here, you believe that what you have been taught to think, feel, and act is the real you. You hold this belief simply because you don't know how to access the higher, better part of yourself. This causes you to defend and try to perfect your patterns, thus taking your focus off your heart and throwing you out of synergy and into avoidance. You must remove these two untruths: that you have to look and act in a way that others would approve in order to be loved, and that you are your patterns. Then you can be honest and look at all the things you do to avoid being in synergy.

Once you believe all the way to a cellular level that you are a God-Being; therefore you don't have to earn Love - you are Loved and you are Love - then it is safe to look all patterns in the face. You are not your patterns! You are really not what you eat, as we are told so often. You are not what you think. You are not what you feel. You are not what you do. You are not who others say you are. Those are simply patterns that are acting as substitutes for the real you. You do have to have patterns to express through but they must support who you really are, not who you really aren't.

The trick then is to stay focused on the fact that you are not any of your patterns expressing through your mental, emotional, and physical.

*You are a God-Being waiting to express.*

That focus totally takes away the need to defend your unreal patterns. It takes away the need to defend your actions, your feelings, your opinions, or for that matter what you eat! If your patterns are *not* supporting the real you, you'll want to know it and you'll want to replace them with new, effective patterns. If they *are* supporting the real you; they are perfect so again there is no need for defense.

Being *in* synergy requires you to be real. While expressing *from* synergy requires you to have patterns that support the real. If you can train your pets, then surely you can train your mental, emotional, and physical. Knowing that these parts of you are trainable means you won't have to hide from the real you when your patterns might possibly look bad. Just be grateful for the opportunity to change the pattern. Remember you are already O.K. You are Love and you are loved.

## *Exercises*

1. The following is a list of a few of the favorite patterns that may be assisting you in avoiding a synergy connect with others' expressions and with your own expressing:

*(List your "favorite" as #1, next favorite as #2, etc. through #4. Then add any other favorites.)*

_____   Judging a person's decision.

_____   Making their issue your emotion.

_____   Saying it isn't appropriate to express myself here.

_____   Deciding how the other person is going to respond before you express so your expression will be appropriate and effective.

_____

_____

_____

_____

_____

_____

_____

_____

_____

_____

2. Look at your list again and note the fears that fuel your avoidance patterns. Talk about the biggest fear with a friend and then affirm a new pattern. Work through as many as you can.

*(Remember every un-owned fear you have makes you dishonest and out of synergy.)*

_____

_____

_____

_____

_____

_____

_____

_____

_____

_____

_____

_____

_____

_____

3. What things have you done in the past or do now that have convinced you that you are not a God Being? Write them down and then write the word PATTERNS across your list. Now tell as many people as it takes for you to believe that you are a God Being, not your patterns.

_____

_____

_____

_____

_____

_____

_____

_____

_____

_____

_____

_____

_____

_____

_____

_____

_____

ℭ𝔯

*You are*

*a God Being,*

*you are not*

*your Patterns!*

ℰ𝔠

## ♥  *Get Things Done Patterns*

Synergy is about flow. Getting things done is about effort. Synergy is about support from the whole universe. Getting things done is about doing it alone. Synergy is about living life abundantly. Getting things done is about lack, even if you get a lot done, because there is no fullness to it.

Life does not have to be lived in the pressured, empty way that most people today live life. The answer is simple, return to your spirit family where Love, Power, and Wisdom exists in great measure; and you have access to all of it.

What are you going to do about all those daily tasks that *have* to be done? In synergy, they become opportunities for expression rather than a *have to*. This takes us back to square one. If, and only if there is a heart's intent, is there a reason to do a task. If there is a heart's intent, then there is a way the synergy of the universe can support you in expressing through a healthy pattern into any form. The daily task being the form and your mental, emotional, and physical bodies providing the healthy patterns.

You have free will. You must define what you want to express, (what is your heart's intent), before you can have the universal support of synergy. You must define how you want to express before you can be aware of unhealthy patterns of expression. It is in the expression part of living that you become powerful. You can know that there is an unhealthy pattern still blocking your expression if you have not created powerfully in the physical after defining your heart's intent.

What would be some healthy patterns in the physical that might support the real you in your daily activities? (Examples: healthy food, deep breathing, good posture.)

_____

_____

_____

_____

_____

_____

_____

What would be some healthy patterns in the emotional that might support the real you in your daily activities? (Examples: allowing yourself to be in Joy because you trust synergy, using upsets to point to an unhealthy pattern.)

_____

_____

_____

_____

_____

_____

_____

_____

What would be healthy patterns in the mental that might support the real you in your daily activities? (Example: holding focus on the intent of your heart.)

_____

_____

_____

_____

_____

_____

_____

If all four bodies; physical, emotional, mental and spiritual are expressing in healthy ways then you are in flow with life. You *are* flow. Your expression from synergy empowers you, as well as empowers your relationships, your creations and the consciousness of the planet.

We exert so much energy getting things done because we work against ourselves rather than support the real us in expressing. No wonder people separate their lives into categories. We call those categories: work (physical), friends (emotional), conversation (mental), growth (spiritual). We separate them because we have never chosen healthy patterns that create a flow through the physical, emotional, mental, and spiritual in every single expression of our lives.

> *If you are to allow synergy to flow through you into your life, then you must have flow through all of your bodies at all times.*

You are a God Being. I am a God Being. We all bring our special gifts to earth. These gifts are gifts of the heart. Our patterns of expression either cancel out these gifts or support them. When you look at an unhealthy pattern it is simply taking an ugly wrapping off a beautiful gift so you can display it appropriately in God's world through a healthy pattern. Synergy won't fit into old "ego patterns". You can't put new wine into old wineskins.

### Relationship Patterns

You can't hide behind language, behaviors, similarities or forms in relationships and stay in synergy.

### Avoidance Patterns

You won't have to avoid the real you once you understand that the mental, emotional, and physical bodies are re-trainable.

### Get Things Done Patterns

You must define what and how the real you wants to express before you can be aware of the empty "get things done" patterns.

## *Exercises*

1. What would you like to give to the person you love most in the whole world?
>    a.) Go to your heart; find the energy or energies that want to be expressed there.
>    b.) Define how you want to express those heart energies.
>    c.) How will you act as if it is so?

It is so in the etheric energies the minute you define. At that point, it is just a matter of waiting to allow the manifestation in to the physical. If it becomes an obligation or impossibility, you have stopped the synergy.

2. List two unhealthy patterns that happen in each of your four bodies when you are feeling pressured. How can you change those to healthy patterns?

*(Remember, to be in synergy you must have flow through all your bodies at all times.)*

## √ *Physical*

_____

_____

_____

_____

_____

_____

## √ *Emotional*

_____

_____

_____

_____

_____

## √ *Mental*

_____

_____

_____

_____

_____

## √ *Spiritual*

_____

_____

_____

_____

_____

3. Think of the person you admire the most.
   a.) Which of their heart expressions do you enjoy?

   _____

   _____

   _____

   _____


   b.) What forms do they use to express those heart
   qualities?

   _____

   _____

   _____

   _____


   c.) What do you like least about that person? Is it a
   pattern?

   _____

   _____

   _____

   _____

   _____

d.) Can you separate the way they are expressing from what they are expressing? Try?

_____

_____

_____

_____

_____

e.) Is there a heart energy present? It helps to set the pattern aside before listening for a heart quality.

_____

_____

_____

_____

_____

_____

_____

_____

_____

_____

_____

f.) The pattern you don't like for them to express through is probably a pattern you have that you don't like in yourself. Check it out. Is it blocking you from synergy because it is unhealthy or because you have been trained to judge it?

_____

_____

_____

_____

_____

_____

_____

_____

_____

_____

_____

_____

_____

_____

_____

ॐ

*If, and only if*

*there is a*

*heart's intent,*

*is there a reason*

*to do a task.*

෫

## *Group Discussion*

1. The first chapter on synergy was about believing that the energy of the heart is the most important, precious, powerful thing in the world. This chapter is about getting rid of the unhealthy patterns in our lives that block the heart gifts from expressing in the world. You can't be part of a synergistic, universal flow if your pipeline is clogged.

*Review a recent day in your life. Check each event to see if the heart was the subject. For those times when you were off the real subject, what feelings were you in? What was your mind saying? What was the task?*

_____

_____

_____

_____

_____

_____

_____

_____

_____

_____

_____

_____

2. An expression is a heart quality that makes its way from your heart as an energy, then travels through your mental, emotional, and physical bodies and out into the world. So, it is easy to see that all of the patterns you express through these bodies must support that heart energy or it can't make it into the world.

*As you read this chapter, which of your expression blocking patterns were you most aware?*

_____

_____

_____

_____

_____

_____

_____

_____

_____

_____

_____

_____

_____

3. If listening is an expression of you, then an energy of the heart must be present while you listen.

*How does the energy get to the other person?*

_____

_____

_____

_____

_____

_____

_____

_____

_____

_____

_____

_____

_____

_____

_____

_____

_____

_____

4. If you are having a conversation expressing from the heart, then your heart and theirs should be in resonance whether you are talking or listening.

*How can this be true if the hearts are expressing different energies? Does it matter?*

*How do your other three bodies, physical, emotional and mental express through listening?*

*Try practicing using listening as an expression.*

_____

_____

_____

_____

_____

_____

_____

_____

_____

_____

_____

_____

_____

_____

5. The more you grow and the higher your vibration becomes; the more dangerous it is to bottleneck. Bottlenecking is where you allow expression in all of your bodies but one, and somehow you just can't seem to let go of your unhealthy pattern(s) of expression in that one space. It is like tying a string around our aura and pulling it in like a corset. From that one chakra space you will start creating very negatively in your world and health.

*What is your bottleneck? Which body? What is the new pattern that will replace the old?*

---

---

---

---

---

---

---

---

---

---

---

---

---

---

---

---

6. A cover-up pattern is when you gush or over express either mentally, emotionally, or physically so that balance is overthrown and flow is stopped.

*What are your cover-up patterns?*

_____

_____

_____

_____

_____

_____

_____

_____

_____

_____

_____

_____

_____

_____

_____

_____

7. It is almost like you were assigned an expression space by your family: you couldn't express more or better than certain people, but you were expected to express more and better than others. Children are lucky when an area of their expression doesn't get an assigned size so they can make it be whatever they want.

*Who assigned your spaces and what did they give you permission to express?*

_____

_____

_____

_____

_____

_____

_____

_____

_____

_____

_____

_____

_____

_____

*What space was carved for you? Take plenty of time to journal about the size of your expression spaces. Are you expected to be less than others or more than others in each? In how many spaces are you just you?*

_____

_____

_____

_____

_____

_____

_____

_____

_____

_____

_____

_____

_____

_____

_____

_____

_____

_____

*What unhealthy patterns do you need to eliminate and what healthy patterns would you like to claim? Give back to your family their limited gifts and thank them for the unlimited ones.*

---

_____

_____

_____

_____

_____

_____

_____

_____

_____

_____

_____

_____

_____

_____

_____

---

*Over the next two weeks continue to observe and journal about the size of your expression spaces. Are they changing?*

8. You may have associated expression with the freedom to choose structures. This is not necessarily so. Your patterns of expression need to be chosen by you. These patterns can fit within already defined structures. The structures aren't as important as you have been lead to believe. It is not possible for you to choose all the rules and regulations on the planet. You live in a physical world with physical laws. There are Universal laws. Laws of the towns. Laws of jobs. In fact every relationship you have should have an agreed upon definition, or law. Those laws or structures are not a limitation to the way you express. A child who has no boundaries is no more free to express than a child who lives with boundaries. It all depends on whether their patterns of expression are healthy or not - that is their freedom.

*Are you free? What structures have you let artificially define your? What are your healthy patterns of expression?*

---

---

---

---

---

---

---

---

---

9. Your expression should flow the same to all people and in all situations. If you are different in any situations then you are acting from ego patterns rather than from real, healthy patterns.

*Who are you in a new social situation?*

_____

_____

_____

_____

_____

_____

*Who are you with your family?*

_____

_____

_____

_____

_____

_____

_____

_____

*Who are you in a romantic situation?*

_____

_____

_____

_____

_____

_____

*Who are you as a guest in someone's home?*

_____

_____

_____

_____

*Who are you when you have company into your home?*

_____

_____

_____

_____

_____

_____

_____

# 5

# Claiming the Energy
of Discernment

To illustrate how you can claim a heart quality and take it all the way through the process to synergy, let's take a look at the energy of Discernment.

Discernment is the ability to tell the difference between things that seem to be opposites but you somehow confuse as similar. You would think that energies as opposite as abundance and lack would not be confused, but without Discernment they can be totally mistaken. Without Discernment you usually live somewhere in the middle of the road. For instance, most people do not allow excessive abuse but they don't expect excessive Honor either. So it becomes quite evident that Discernment is the key to that "life promotion" for which you have been waiting. It opens the door to what is best for you. It sorts out all the chaff and leaves your mind and emotions clear of confusion and attachment.

Since Discernment is a heart quality, you need to ask for it, meditate on it and desire it in the core of your being. Then you will have a new piece in your spiritual repertoire. Discernment also helps you to understand the difference between such things as what is real vs. judgment from the ego, or focus vs. fixation. To most people the range of difference between those two ends seems to be only an inch or two, while in the reality of Discernment it is a mile. Because many of us were never introduced to Discernment while growing up, our comfort zone in receiving it may be a bit shallow at first. But that comfort zone hopefully will grow with use of the information and exercises in this book.

This chapter is intended to intensify your awareness around:

1. Celebration vs. denial  (emotional)
2. "What-is" vs. judgment  (mental)
3. Honor vs. abuse  (physical)

## ♥ Celebration vs. Denial

Celebration is having positive emotions about who you are - celebrating the expression of your heart, no matter what size the expression. Of course, since we are all spiritual beings, that means your emotional response is to the energy of *who* you are rather than to the action of *what* you do. It is the same for the other person. You are to celebrate who they are, not what they do. Denial, on the other hand, focuses on what you do and denies that you are the energies of the heart.

It is true that your heart gets expressed in the physical world, but it should have already been celebrated inside of you before the physical manifestation.

You may have a hard time celebrating the heart when

judgment and punishment seem ever present in the world. So you shrink back inside of yourself and do not celebrate who you are, so that you won't have to risk getting out of your comfort zone of safe patterns. You falsely believe that if you ignore who you are then maybe others won't notice you and judge you. It takes a lot of courage to celebrate who you are when "the world" is looking for cracks in your armor. In fact it is a lot easier to get sympathy than to be celebrated.

So you hide and you wait, but what are you waiting for? Are you waiting for permission, for the world to grow up, or for your friends and partner to celebrate you first?

Denial says that you can celebrate, but only if everything turns out well and people approve. Then it is safe and you have permission to be celebrated. The outcome is the key to who you are when you are in denial. Let's look closer at this slippery concept. Do you applaud a child for being or for "getting it right"? Do you see people as successful when they have expressed a lot or done a lot? Do you look at other's hearts or their accumulation of things? The interesting irony of all this is that getting it right, getting a lot done and accumulating things, may be the end product of celebration, but you can't work from the outside in, you have to *be* first and then *do*. If you start being conscious of the energy (or person) behind the well-done job, then you will also start being more aware of the real you behind the doing.

Students of metaphysics get so upset when the symbols of their life; like getting sick, or having their car break down, are "bad". They say, "What did I *do* wrong?" They did nothing wrong. They simply forgot to celebrate who they were.

*If you celebrate yourself as heart energies, then happenings are just symbols, not tragedies or successes.*

Breaking the habit of continually looking at your doing is a tough one. You beat up on yourself, judge yourself, punish yourself, lie, manipulate and cheat simply because you are in denial rather than celebration.

There are many patterns of response that you will have to change to allow Discernment to enter into the celebration/denial arena. One simple way to make space for Discernment is to share in your journal, or with a friend, who you were during the day rather than what you got done or what kind of victim you got to play out. Another way to create space for Discernment is as mentioned before; ask yourself who is the other person *being* and comment on that rather than limit your conversation to how good they look or what a great job they did. For example: you might say, "That outfit really expresses your Beauty well", or you could comment on a job well done by saying, "Your Persistence was amazing while you were laying the stone walkway." As you can see, a change will happen in what draws your attention and how you conduct your conversations. It won't take too long to discover if you, or anyone else for that matter, have Discernment in the area of celebration vs. denial.

Celebration will be happening all the time when you are able to discern the real energy from the forms. This celebration is not a hip-hip-hurrah, but an alive feeling. When you feel alive it is because you have discovered what holds meaning and is real in the world. Forms become a support system like the adjectives to a subject.

Celebration doesn't mean you can't have upset feelings at the same time. It is an expansion of the emotions so that you can be in growth and manifestation all at once. The so-called "negative" emotions tell you that a heart quality is missing; thus they help you to grow. The so-called "positive" emotions motivate you to express in the world; thus they are part of the manifestation side of your spiritual energy cycle.

ᘯ

*Celebration will be*

*happening all the time*

*when you are able*

*to discern*

*the real energy*

*from the forms.*

ᘰ

## *Exercises*

1. What are some of the heart qualities you express in your doing?

*Look at one household chore and personal care item you do every day, and one family relationship.*

Household Chore:

_____

_____

_____

_____

Personal Care Item:

_____

_____

_____

_____

Family Relationship:

_____

_____

_____

_____

_____

2. Next, compare how you are now to how you were when you did these in your childhood. Are you more aware now or then?

_____

_____

_____

_____

_____

_____

3. How can you change your conversations to talk from celebration rather than denial? Practice now by pretending to share with your mother in a way that celebrates who she is around cooking.

_____

_____

_____

_____

_____

_____

_____

4. How can you emotionally celebrate and deal with your fears at the same time? Work with both sides of the emotions with the energy of Play. What fears do you still have and what pieces have you claimed to celebrate?

_____

_____

_____

_____

_____

_____

5. In what areas of your life do you create denial by putting your attention and values only on the doing? Is this habit or is there a fear of being real lurking nearby?

_____

_____

_____

_____

_____

_____

_____

6. How do you "punish" yourself when you are in denial? (By criticizing yourself, working too hard, stopping the flow in your life?) How could you stop the punishment?

_____

_____

_____

_____

_____

_____

_____

_____

_____

_____

_____

_____

_____

_____

_____

_____

7. Write down all the "bad" things that have happened in your life. Now write the word DENIAL across them. Remember there is no success or failure when you are focused on the energy – Celebrate! All happenings are just symbols.

_____

_____

_____

_____

_____

_____

_____

_____

_____

_____

_____

_____

_____

_____

_____

_____

_____

8. Write down who you are right now (heart qualities) as a spirit being. Write the word CELEBRATE across them.

_____

_____

_____

_____

_____

_____

_____

_____

_____

_____

_____

_____

_____

_____

_____

_____

_____

_____

9. Take the worst scenario you can think of and make a success story out of it. (Don't change the events, just change your values.)

_____

_____

_____

_____

_____

_____

_____

_____

_____

_____

_____

_____

_____

_____

_____

CR

*Discernment is the*

*ability to tell*

*the difference between*

*things that seem*

*to be opposites*

*but you somehow*

*confuse as similar.*

EÒ

♥  *"What-is" vs. Judgment:*

Being able to see the "what-is" of a situation means you have developed a healthy mental adult and a self-confident mental child. If you are in the state of "what-is-ness" you know when a situation or statement is totally coming from the ego or totally coming from the heart, no question about it.

A good example of "what-is" vs. judgment occurred not too long ago between a friend and myself. This friend and I had a telephone relationship for years but rarely ever got together to visit in person. After I moved from Atlanta to North Carolina, she started saying how much she missed seeing me. The truth of the situation is that she couldn't possibly miss what she never had. However, her fearful ego self believed she could no longer access me if she needed me so she started to emotionally cling and her mind went into judgment.

If I were to say my friend spoke an untruth but I knew that it was her ego speaking, how can she be judged? The real person wasn't doing the speaking. If, on the other hand, I say she doesn't really miss me she misses the crutch I might provide; again there can be no judgment because that is just a what-is. Without judgment, I am free to look and see if any real exists. I can then see that there is a small piece of Community that resonates between our hearts.

Separation between patterns (ego) and the heart (realness) is the end product of Discernment used through the mental body. As you may have already guessed, there aren't too many healthy mental bodied people out there. Most folks use their mental bodies for judgment of patterns. Usually conversations are based on judgment.

Actions become doing against your heart rather than

doing from your heart because of judgment. Emotions are often pulled along by judgment. Most of the television news broadcasts are a judgment. Many politicians get elected because they impress us with what they are going to do; not with who they are as a person. It is all empty! Judgment should be banished from our realities. If the mental body is unable to separate your heart from your ego it is unhealthy.

*The sole job of the mental body is to hold focus on definitions of the heart.*

"What-is" is necessary. Judgment is not necessary. Judgment does not connect us to people. It does not protect us from people. It is wasted time and energy. Plus it is probably the most destructive weapon in the world. People should have to register all their judgments! They are much worse than guns. The judgment bullets become psychic attacks on people's auras. They poison the air of our mass consciousness, and they keep you personally from being real.

Discernment brings the clarity of separation to "what-is" vs. judgment. "What-is" can then be said with out any emotional reaction or loss of mental focus because it is about what is real. "What-is" can never be used against anyone else including yourself. When you bring Discernment to your mental body it keeps you from trying to connect to those people you can't be connected to because they are in their ego. In addition, it protects you from all those situations that had the illusion of danger when you were in your ego. Discernment is a must if you intend to use your mental body at all.

Giving up judgment doesn't mean you give up action against wrongs. But you do it from a different place. You can correct situations and still Love. You can act without the motivation of anger or fear. You can take action and let it go instead of brood over it for a week or two.

## *Exercises*

1. Judgment comes from ego so it blocks you from seeing realness. What would happen to your life if you started thinking in terms of "what-is"?

_____

_____

_____

_____

_____

_____

_____

_____

_____

_____

_____

_____

_____

_____

_____

_____

_____

_____

2. In which of the following situations do your judgments come up?

*Remember, if you are in emotional reaction, your mental body is being guided by judgments rather than by the Discernment of your heart.*

    a.) You are grocery shopping when you hear someone speak in an angry voice to his or her child.

_____

_____

_____

_____

_____

_____

    b. ) Your neighbor's dog is so thin that it looks as though it has not been fed in weeks.

_____

_____

_____

_____

_____

_____

_____

c.) Your relative is rigid in their belief system and argues with you about their rightness.

_____

_____

_____

_____

_____

d.) A friend never offers to pay your way even though you pay theirs often.

_____

_____

_____

_____

_____

e.) A couple brought their child to the movie-theater and he persistently kicked the back of your seat.

_____

_____

_____

_____

_____

_____

f.) A new Mercedes is parked at the far empty end of the mall parking lot.

_____

_____

_____

_____

_____

3. You have company in your home. What will you talk about if judgment is not allowed? Can you stop their judgment?

_____

_____

_____

_____

_____

_____

_____

_____

_____

_____

_____

_____

4. Name a "what-is" lesson you have had on your growth path recently. Did you start with judgment and then move to a "what-is" or did you skip the judgment altogether?

_____

_____

_____

_____

_____

_____

_____

_____

_____

_____

_____

_____

_____

_____

_____

_____

_____

_____

5. Is there anyone you feel connected to powerfully when you are not with them physically, such as talking to them on the phone? These people are heart connects with whom it will be easiest to focus on the "what-is".

_____

_____

_____

_____

_____

_____

6. If the new message you give your mental body is to listen to the heart, then how can you be protected against verbal attacks?

_____

_____

_____

_____

_____

_____

_____

_____

How about someone's psychic, behind-the-scenes attacks?

_____

_____

_____

_____

Will you be more aware of them and better able to confront if you are real?

_____

_____

_____

_____

7. If being in a judgment takes away Discernment, why have we come to rely on it so heavily? Why did your family use it?

_____

_____

_____

_____

_____

_____

_____

_____

8. What constitutes a healthy mental adult? How does it parent a judgmental mental child?

_____

_____

_____

_____

_____

_____

_____

_____

9. What does a healthy mental child look like?

_____

_____

_____

_____

_____

_____

_____

### ♥ *Honor vs. Abuse*

Either Honor or abuse happens constantly in every one of your bodies - spiritual, mental, emotional, or physical. I am going to focus on the physical. In fact I could fill an entire book looking at the subject of Honor vs. abuse. The physical body is the one we think we are most aware of and in truth it is probably where we are least aware.

You are abusing your physical every time you don't use Discernment to own and release an emotion and it gets stored in your body. You are abusing your physical every time you don't use Discernment in your mental and you store the judgment, or untruth, in your physical body. You abuse your body every time awareness is absent anywhere inside of you. However, you also abuse yourself when your awareness is absent outside of you. Discernment brought into the physical helps to heighten awareness there. You are then able to bring your full consciousness into everything you do. You become aware of that dishwasher door that was left down, even in the dark, if you have the Discernment gift. You are aware of the other cars, the landscape, your car, and your body while driving down the highway.

> *You are only honoring your physical body when your heart energy is brought into your physical world.*

This means you must bring awareness of who you are being into the physical every single moment of your day.

It is amazing how much time we spend on a physical job and how little physical awareness we bring to it. Our mind wanders off into judgment. Our emotions go off on their tangent. Our psychic part wanders off in a fantasy. Face it, most of us don't like living in the physical world. We try beating it into submission so that it will give us what we want, but we don't Honor it by giving it awareness. Anything short of full awareness in the physical is abuse.

This doesn't mean you have to give up feeling or thinking to devote your whole self to physical awareness. It isn't an either/or choice, but an expansion of awareness. This is impossible without the support of your good friend Discernment. Discernment literally creates a space in the physical for your energy to flow into. Let's do it right now.

> First claim that you have Discernment.......Now imagine yourself to be a circle beyond your flesh and bones........Feel your energy expanding into it........Be aware of what that space is touching, feeling, or seeing...........

That is really all you have to do. It is this gift that helps you receive from life as well as give to life.

Discernment brought into your physical world to heighten your awareness is essential if we are to heal the planet. How can we bring change to a place where we have no awareness?

## *Exercises*

1. Dishonoring one's physical body by abusing food is seen as a reward by many people. Why?

_____

_____

_____

_____

_____

_____

_____

_____

2. What does it mean to make an awareness space, or to be present in the physical? What is your biggest block to doing that?

_____

_____

_____

_____

_____

_____

_____

3. Once you bring your awareness into the physical, will you automatically Honor the physical?

_____

_____

_____

_____

_____

How are you going to increase your awareness?

_____

_____

_____

_____

_____

_____

_____

_____

_____

_____

How can you stop old patterns of unawareness?

_____

_____

_____

_____

_____

_____

_____

_____

4. How many of your celebrations that we talked about earlier, Persistence, Nurturing, and Support, have a real, defined space in the physical?

_____

_____

_____

_____

_____

_____

_____

_____

5. Do you define and set boundaries that are Honoring; i.e., to let your real-self express, or are your boundaries abusive because they shut out your realness? How do you enforce them?

_____

_____

_____

_____

_____

_____

_____

_____

_____

_____

_____

_____

_____

_____

_____

_____

_____

6. What is your physical awareness quotient?

   a.) Do you make sure your feet are clean when you enter someone's house?

   b.) Do you let your kids run wild while in someone else's space?

   c.)  Are you sensitive to what another person is doing when you enter their space?

   d.) Do you eat when you are hungry?

   e.) Do you rest when you are tired?

   f.) Are you appreciative of nature every day?

   g.) Do know when your body needs water?

   h.) Do you know when you are frowning?

7. Do you view your minute to minute space as an energy exchange place?

_____

_____

_____

_____

How can that be a reality?

_____

_____

_____

_____

_____

_____

_____

_____

_____

_____

_____

_____

_____

What do you see as the purpose of your physical being?

_____

_____

_____

_____

_____

_____

_____

_____

8. Does the size of your physical awareness affect your giving and receiving cycle?

_____

_____

_____

_____

_____

_____

_____

9. What does it look like to allow dishonor in your space? Is just any interaction in the physical without an energy exchange a dishonor?

_____

_____

_____

_____

_____

_____

_____

_____

_____

_____

_____

_____

_____

_____

_____

_____

As your heart moves through your mental, emotional, and physical bodies into the world, you become more and the world becomes more. When your mental body is focused on the realness of the heart, you define your world rather than judge it. When your emotional body is trained to celebrate the energy of the heart, reacting to life will be a thing of the past. When the physical body is handed the ball of heart energy that has passed from the heart to the mental, to the emotional then to the physical, you then get to live in total awareness. To be present and alive is your birthright, why not claim it?

> *You can only be in synergy by claiming your birthright - to be part of the whole.*

> *Each heart quality participates in your wholeness.*

Each heart quality is just as powerful as Discernment, but Discernment is an invaluable tool in this whole process. As you have discovered from doing these exercises, Discernment helps you sort out what is real energy and what is unreal energy. Thus, it lets you see beyond words and forms to the heart. It also supports you in living from your heart by holding the truth up for you to read clearly at all times. Discernment is definitely a friend.

CR

*You are abusing*

*your physical*

*every time you don't*

*use Discernment*

*to own and release*

*an emotion.*

EO

## *Group Discussion*

1. Share with a member of the group about who you are around Persistence, Nurturing, and Support without telling them what forms you use to express those energies.

_____

_____

_____

_____

_____

_____

_____

_____

2. Now pick an energy/heart quality (from the list of heart qualities at the end of the book).

*Describe the forms that you express the energy through, and see if the group can uncover the energy.*

_____

_____

_____

_____

_____

3. Discernment is like a flashlight shining in a dark room. It brings clarity to whatever it shines on.

*What are the things that cut off your light? Or keep you from turning it on?*

_____

_____

_____

_____

_____

_____

_____

_____

_____

_____

_____

_____

_____

_____

_____

_____

_____

4. Most of us were trained at a very young age to use our minds for judgment. Even when we say we are speaking our truth, it is usually just an assessment of what is going on. You can't read someone's heart through his or her mind, emotions, or actions. You can only read their heart through their heart. There can never be judgment of the heart.

*In what areas of your life is judgment a problem?*

_____

_____

_____

_____

_____

_____

_____

_____

_____

_____

_____

_____

_____

_____

_____

_____

_____

5. Focus on whether your emotions drag your mind around or your mind drags your emotions around.

*How can you stop circling and get back on course?*

_____

_____

_____

_____

_____

_____

_____

_____

_____

_____

_____

_____

_____

_____

_____

6. A dark spot on the lens of Discernment is using words to get someone to do, think, or feel something you want and bypass their heart. This is called manipulation.

*How do your word patterns manipulate?*

_____

_____

_____

_____

_____

_____

_____

_____

_____

_____

_____

_____

_____

_____

_____

_____

_____

7. The heart is for life, not against it. It supports what is good, it does not focus on what is wrong -- (this doesn't mean we don't see the truth of what-is and deal with it.) The heart doesn't need to "fix" anybody because it approaches everyone with Acceptance. Fears are separated and are seen clearly as being outside of the heart. It always makes a space for others hearts even when they are acting from their nastiest patterns.

*What are some of your new patterns of thinking that are guided by your heart?*

_____

_____

_____

_____

_____

_____

_____

_____

_____

_____

_____

_____

_____

8. You need to learn to ask, "Is any one "home" to be celebrated?" Since you have now trained the mind to not take over and judge whether they are "home" or not by their performance; you are free to make it a 'what is' if they are lacking what is needed for that task or situation. What if, for instance, a job needs to be done and a co-worker has no Persistence. They appear to be lazy and seem like they are not carrying their load. You may ask them to do another task or even fire them, but if they brought anything real to the job, like a moment of Creativity, your emotions can celebrate.

*How can you re-train your emotions so they will be capable of celebration?*

9. To be real you must celebrate not only what heart energy is being expressed, but also the size of it. Don't forget, the heart subject can be heard even in the midst of emotional upset – they are not one and the same.

*Can you be real while others are unreal?*

*Can you hold an upset feeling and a celebration feeling at the same time?*

*How do you know what subject the heart is trying to present?*

*How can a heart energy be measured?*

_____

_____

_____

_____

_____

_____

_____

_____

_____

_____

_____

_____

_____

10. A big piece of Honor is understanding and using boundaries correctly. Most people fall into one of two categories:

Category #1 fits everyone who holds such rigid boundaries that no one is allowed into their life.

Category #2 includes all those people who invade others' spaces and allow theirs to be treated the same way.

Boundaries are for the purpose of keeping out everything that can't be celebrated.

*Which category do you work from?*

_____

_____

_____

_____

_____

_____

*How much of the time do you set boundaries that Honor who you are?*

_____

_____

_____

_____

_____

_____

*Name at least two boundaries you need to re-define.*

# 6

# More on Discernment

You can now see how taking a heart quality, such as Discernment, and letting it re-train and instruct each of your three lower bodies (mental, emotional, physical) puts you well on your way to ultimate spirituality. Well, it takes you at least half way. The other half happens when you expand that energy by connecting with the synergy of all other hearts. You must first understand who you are as heart energies to finally understand we are all one.

In this chapter we are going to look at three areas where Discernment is already changing your life - if you have been applying it:

1.  Process vs. Upset  (emotional)
2.  Focus vs. Fixation  (mental)
3.  Abundance vs. Lack  (physical)

♥ *Process vs. Upset*

A major act in your life is the process of:
1. Giving feelings a voice and listening to them.
2. Sorting out which ones are about you and which are about others.
3. Hearing what is your truth underneath a feeling.
4. Clearing out the feeling so you will have space to act on your truth.
5. Becoming that new truth.

You can go to therapy, read books and take classes to learn how to do each step of this process. You can ask support from others to keep you from slipping and sliding around in the process. You can journal to stay with the process. But without discernment you may not even realize you need to have a process. Emotional upset can unknowingly become part of your life; something you just live with. In the absence of emotional discernment, you can't be on a spiritual growth path.

We have already talked about some of the attributes of Discernment. Such as what is real and what is unreal, taking judgment out of the picture, making life a celebration, and expanding awareness so you can be bigger in the world. Think about it for a minute. If all of that is really in play, how much upset will there be? None. However, upset does happen so let's look at how you can get pulled off your process into upset.

Often times it seems you are pulled off your process (i.e., the path to your truth), when upset hits; but in reality you are first pulled off your process and then become an easy prey of upset. Upset is more than just being emotionally attached or emotionally out of balance around a happening. It is more than just intensity or endurance of feeling.

*Upset is the absence of Discernment in your emotional body.*

It is that out of focus place where you can't tell what is pattern and what is heart. In fact, upset can keep you out of process for weeks, years, or even lifetimes.

In the case of Sue and John, upset took over and "process" in regard to their relationship was never regained. Sue had an affair with John's best friend. John found out and proceeded to have an affair with Sue's best friend. Their anger turned to blame. The blame turned into a physical battle over their children and belongings. These two loving, caring people turned into vindictive, non-heartful people. The battle lost its intensity after a few years but all the heart energies they had shared were aborted and left wrapped in upset. Had they moved through their anger to the heart, this experience could have been part of their process in becoming more rather than less.

Discernment is a tool for bringing you back to focus on your path of process. Since the emotional process always takes you to your heart, then the absence of it would mean your daily tasks and interactions would lack celebration. Your path of emotional upset might not seem too disturbing to you if you never experienced living totally from the heart. But once you have accepted that there is choice, through the gift of discernment, you will be totally unwilling to ever stay away from the heart path again.

ᘓ

*Discernment is*

*a tool for bringing*

*you back to focus*

*on your path*

*of process.*

ᘛ

## *Exercises*

1. If your emotional body's purpose is to constantly remind you that you are in need of a heart energy, how can you be aware of your feeling response every minute of the day so you don't get stuck in upset?

_____

_____

_____

_____

_____

_____

_____

_____

_____

_____

_____

_____

_____

_____

_____

2. How do you deal with your lesson feelings and your celebration feelings differently?

_____

_____

_____

_____

_____

_____

_____

_____

_____

_____

_____

_____

_____

_____

_____

_____

_____

_____

_____

3. What "tools" of emotional support could you use to empower your process of listening to, owning, and releasing your emotions?

_____

_____

_____

_____

_____

_____

_____

_____

_____

_____

_____

_____

_____

_____

_____

_____

_____

4. Can you hear the heart before you clear all the emotion?

_____

_____

_____

_____

_____

_____

_____

_____

5. How do you know when your heart is speaking? Do you confuse it with your emotions?

_____

_____

_____

_____

_____

_____

_____

_____

6. What supports do you use to hear the heart voice more clearly and consistently? Name at least two you aren't presently using.

_____

_____

_____

_____

_____

_____

_____

_____

_____

_____

_____

_____

_____

_____

_____

_____

_____

7. What is upset? Is it always a strong emotion? Can emotional shut down be upset? What is your favorite way to be upset?

_____

_____

_____

_____

_____

_____

_____

_____

_____

_____

_____

_____

_____

_____

_____

_____

_____

8. What "tools" could you use to get out of upset? (Is Discernment one of your tools?)

_____

_____

_____

_____

_____

_____

_____

_____

_____

_____

_____

_____

_____

_____

_____

_____

_____

_____

_____

CR

*Your emotional body's*

*purpose is to*

*constantly remind you*

*that you are*

*in need of*

*a heart energy.*

EC

## ♥ *Focus vs. Fixation*

Focus is different than holding a space for physical awareness. It is different than zeroing in on an idea. It is more than staying with your emotional process.

*Focus is the journey to, and the journey from, your heart's expression.*

The journey begins by listening to the emotions that are telling you that you are missing something (something inside). Your mind must hold the light at the end of the tunnel while you are going through the emotion or you are likely to get stuck in a quagmire of feelings. It continually holds focus on the heart. Once you reach the heart, the mind, still holding focus on the heart, creates a pathway for the new little heart quality to make its way through the "what-is" of life to be celebrated on its way into the world to be expressed.

Fixation is simply a state of being stuck. It is sticking like glue to someone or something outside of your heart. For instance, some of us get so fixated on making a relationship work that we can't focus inside. For some it is our need to appear perfect in the world that becomes a fixation. I know one woman who is fixated on getting what she wants. Her life is literally one big manipulation towards that end. For instance, when she meets someone she doesn't listen to the heart to see what the relationship looks like, but proceeds to charm the newcomer into liking and trusting her. She then proceeds to charmingly pull information, talents, and gifts from her new victim. Her belief that manipulation is Power has her fixated in life. She is stuck in the little space of preying on victims.

But don't make the mistake of thinking only the outside

world causes stuckness or fixation. No, no, no, the inside can be a culprit too. You can be fixated on a small truth that you have outgrown, or it might be on a feeling you have about something or someone. Fixation definitely can take over, either inside or out. You can be fixated on your work, your health, even obsess to the point of fixation about your looks.

> *A fixation is anything that keeps you from focusing on the journey to the heart, then on out through the bodies to gift the world.*

Focus, on the other hand, is the mental body's job of directing that journey.

So where does Discernment come in? Remember what you have learned about Discernment thus far? It sweeps the unreal out of the way and expands awareness of the real to create bigger, clearer spaces. It will be absolutely necessary to have Discernment clear and pave the path for focus to birth your little baby heart qualities.

The confusing piece in all this is that you may tend to assign Discernment to the psychic part of you when in fact it is a function of the heart.

Let's say you went to a psychic to tell you if the person you just met is right for you, or try to intuit what that person is like before you accept a second date. It is the heart that holds that answer. The psychic part of you may figure out the total personality and list good and bad qualities, but you still wouldn't know if this is right for you unless the heart speaks up.

Now this doesn't mean Discernment can't support your intuition, but they are not one and the same. The psychic realm is the misty of possibilities. You can't let it be the voice of your heart. The heart must speak for itself. Focus can't work with many possibilities. It works as the carrier of one piece at a time. Discernment clears the way, it does not make the choice. The heart makes the choice.

CR

*Your mental body's*

*purpose is to*

*holds focus*

*on the heart*

*while you are going*

*through an emotion.*

BD

## *Exercises*

1. What is fixation?

_____

_____

_____

_____

_____

_____

_____

2. List your present outside focuses. Which of these are fixations? Why or why not?

_____

_____

_____

_____

_____

_____

_____

3. What do you fear would happen to you if you stopped focusing outside of you? Pick two areas of your life to look at.

_____

_____

_____

_____

_____

_____

_____

_____

_____

_____

_____

_____

_____

_____

_____

_____

_____

_____

4. What is the role of the mental body? How is your mental body now functioning in each step of its journey?

_____

_____

_____

_____

_____

_____

_____

_____

_____

_____

_____

_____

_____

_____

_____

_____

_____

_____

_____

5. Which side of the heart's journey, going to or from the heart, is easiest for you? Which is your stumbling block? What are some possible solutions?

_____

_____

_____

_____

_____

_____

_____

_____

_____

_____

_____

_____

_____

_____

_____

_____

_____

_____

6. How is Discernment different than psychic ability? Which are you using to get your answers?

_____

_____

_____

_____

_____

_____

_____

_____

_____

_____

_____

_____

_____

_____

_____

_____

_____

7. If the mental body is focused on the heart, how can you have conversations? How can you get things done and do that? What are your trouble spots?

_____

_____

_____

_____

_____

_____

_____

_____

_____

_____

_____

_____

_____

_____

_____

_____

_____

_____

8. Has your language changed to speak of heart energies? With whom do you get the most practice?

_____

_____

_____

_____

_____

_____

_____

_____

_____

_____

_____

_____

_____

_____

_____

_____

_____

_____

୨

*Discernment sweeps*

*the unreal out of*

*the way and*

*expands awareness*

*of the real*

*to create*

*bigger, clearer spaces.*

୧

## ♥ *Abundance vs. Lack*

*Abundance is giving who you are, through what you have, with blessing and intent to gift the world.*

At the same time you can expect and allow your gift to come back to you - multiplied.

Lack happens when you don't give from the heart. You may be giving what you don't have, i.e. from empty coffers. You may be giving but are unwilling to receive. You may be giving to empty places where there is no hope of return. Or you may forget to give your gift as a blessing to the world.

Abundance basically means a healthy giving and receiving cycle with a little blessing and intent thrown in so that your gifts come back multiplied. Discernment helps that cycle happen by increasing your physical awareness and thus increasing the size of your giving and receiving space.

If your giving has to make it to the physical to become an expression, or put another way, a gift to the world; then it can only express as big as your physical awareness space, (this was talked about before under Honor vs. Abuse). If you send out a small gift with blessing and intent it will come back bigger, but can you receive it if your space is still small?

Unfortunately, you may miss a lot of gifts given to you. Discernment can help you expand awareness in your physical space and the size will automatically follow. But there is one little catch, you will have to be willing to clean out the debris that your fears and judgments have created so your space will be clear to send and receive. Discernment lets you see clearly the size and quality of your space, as well as others.

*As you allow any heart quality to grow in your life, you have more pieces that can be joined in synergy across the planet.*

It is like we all get to hold hands. It is one thing to want to have abundance in your life and quite another to decide to willingly give all that you are through what you have, to gift the world. Yet it takes energetically holding hands across the planet to have the biggest possible space. This is true abundance.

Blessing what we have to give is quite different than what is normally seen in the world. The majority of people, even wealthy people, are always wanting more of just about everything. They believe they can only be truly grateful when they have more. They "bless" what they don't have rather than what they have. This results in the energy of lack. The size of their giving and receiving heart space is small. They may accumulate things, but they can't grow spiritually unless their heart energy is allowed to be empowered by expressing into the world. It is through this empowerment that energy flows back to us in abundance.

You can now see how important it is to have a big uncluttered physical space. This not only facilitates flow, growth and abundance personally; but it takes you out of the smallness of a separate non-synergy space and allows you to be a universal being.

Discernment is a wonderful tool for surveying the size and content of your space. It can tell you if you have collected and blessed objects, or even people, rather than heart gifts. It can make you aware when you are giving with no return; thus no flow. It can make you aware of all that you are giving without a blessing. Discernment can also make your giving and receiving cycle intentional. Definition is important both in giving and receiving so that the heart has direction in its flow.

ß

*Lack happens*

*when you*

*don't give*

*from*

*the heart.*

ß

## *Exercises*

1. Do you consider yourself a gift to the world? In what places and at what times? What is the culprit that stops you from being a gift at all times?

_____

_____

_____

_____

_____

_____

_____

_____

_____

_____

_____

_____

_____

_____

_____

_____

_____

2. How could you bless your expression into the physical?

_____

_____

_____

_____

_____

_____

_____

_____

_____

_____

_____

_____

_____

_____

_____

_____

_____

_____

_____

3. How does intent change your gift? Can you have intent, or definition, in both giving and receiving?

_____

_____

_____

_____

_____

_____

_____

_____

_____

_____

_____

_____

_____

_____

_____

_____

_____

_____

_____

_____

4. It was stated that Discernment increases your physical awareness. How much Abundance can you imagine? Are you willing to be aware equal to that size?

_____

_____

_____

_____

_____

_____

5. Do you receive as much as you give?

_____

_____

_____

_____

_____

_____

_____

_____

_____

6. What is your receiving process?

_____

_____

_____

_____

_____

_____

_____

_____

_____

7. How is it possible for energy to come back multiplied?

_____

_____

_____

_____

_____

_____

_____

_____

_____

8. What happens, energetically, if you spend money you don't have? Will this kind of spending create more or create lack?

_____

_____

_____

_____

_____

_____

_____

_____

_____

_____

_____

_____

_____

_____

_____

_____

_____

_____

_____

9. What if you receive when you haven't given?

_____

_____

_____

_____

_____

_____

_____

_____

_____

_____

_____

_____

_____

_____

_____

_____

_____

_____

10. Can you prostitute a heart-energy? How?

_____

_____

_____

_____

_____

_____

_____

_____

_____

_____

_____

_____

_____

_____

_____

_____

_____

_____

11. How can you give knowing you can receive multiplied, and not get caught in the selfish web of giving in order to receive?

_____

_____

_____

_____

_____

_____

_____

_____

_____

_____

_____

_____

_____

_____

_____

_____

_____

CR

*Discernment*

*can change*

*your life,*

*if you*

*apply it.*

EC

## *Group Discussion*

1. Upset is the lack of Discernment in the emotional body. It is that out-of-focus place where you can't tell the difference between what life is telling you and what the heart is telling you. Without Discernment you may not even know you are upset.

*Is this less of a problem for you now that you are using the heart energy of Discernment?*

_____

_____

_____

_____

_____

_____

_____

_____

_____

_____

_____

_____

_____

2. Attachment to a person, job, opinion, way-of-life, anything that has become your end goal creates emotional upset. It may be a quiet undercurrent you have become accustomed to or a raging passion you stand on a podium and shout about. Both are upsets. Your emotional body has been taken out of the process of listening to the heart's desire to birth a heart energy.

*What are your primary attachments?*

*Which are quiet undercurrents and which are raging passions?*

_____

_____

_____

_____

_____

_____

_____

_____

_____

_____

_____

_____

_____

_____

3. A victimizer is a person who sees someone else as broken. They put a psychic cage around the other person that says this is not your lesson but your weakness. From that place every emotion or even lack of emotion is emotional upset.

*Give an example of replacing your victimizer upsets with the thought, "I will let you have your lesson".*

_____

_____

_____

_____

_____

_____

_____

_____

_____

_____

_____

_____

_____

_____

_____

4. The mental body's job is to always stay focused on the heart. It is responsible for holding that focus in the midst of physical activity, emotional activity, and mental activity. Fixation occurs when your focus gets attached to anything outside of your heart. Such as, "will they think I am stupid?" "Will they think I am ugly?" "Will they think I am weird?" "Will they like me?" "Will they think I am special?"

*Do you feel your heart is special enough to be the central focus?*

---

---

---

---

---

---

---

---

---

---

---

---

---

5. Does the tiny phrase, "Is it appropriate?" put you into automatic role playing or automatic rebellion? It implies that some special behavior is expected of you from the outside. The heart's definition will be more than appropriate; it will be real. The heart will never violate another living thing. Appropriate was initiated because the heart was forgotten and civilized behavior had to be maintained.

*Are you ready to return to the heart and give up your appropriate list?*

_____

_____

_____

_____

_____

_____

_____

_____

_____

_____

_____

_____

6. There are baby heart qualities that seem so small and fragile you may tend to protect them or be embarrassed by their smallness. It is important to remember that all gifts of spirit are sacred gifts, which have been entrusted to you to share with the world.

*What baby heart quality are you needing to nurture and allow expression?*

*You claim Abundance by growing up your "babies".*

_____

_____

_____

_____

_____

_____

_____

_____

_____

_____

_____

_____

_____

7. You can receive more than you give once you recognize the sacredness of your gift. When you see your gifts as sacred, you also see them belonging to the sacred whole. Once you accept that they belong to that sacred synergy then Abundance is yours. The Abundance that you then receive makes you more. Then you start the whole process over from a bigger space. It is the gift that won't stop giving.

*What is your Abundance quotient?*

_____

_____

_____

_____

_____

_____

_____

_____

_____

_____

_____

_____

_____

_____

CR

*You can receive*

*more than you give*

*once you recognize*

*the sacredness of*

*your gift.*

RO

# 7

# The Ultimate Spiritual Journey

To reach your ultimate spirituality you have to make the world be about your needs. Not in the selfish, self-center way that most people meet their needs; but from the heart. Take the basic need for food. If you really listen to your body, you will discover that there are different hungers. Behind each hunger you will find a heart energy that is the real need. But you will have to learn to go past the physical to the heart. For instance, you may need the spiritual heart energy of Endurance. If you only hear that need in the physical, you may run and get a cup of coffee. However, if you hear the physical as simply a reminder that the heart has a need it wants to fill in your life, then the energy of Endurance will take over and guide you in finding the right food to support the energy of Endurance.

Emotional needs are really heart needs also. Let's say you are upset because your partner or friend isn't very Nurturing. They seem to be oblivious to how life is impacting you. If only they would just bring you a bowl of soup or say a word of sympathy, but they haven't. You have two choices: stay in the emotional need and feel sorry for yourself, or go to the place where the need can have the Power to be met, the heart.

*Once you make it to the energy in the heart, it can then begin its magnetic Power.*

First of all, you will now have Nurturing in and for yourself, but secondly you will now pull it from those around you or someone else will appear bringing the gift of Nurturing.

The same is true for all those mental needs. When a decision comes up for review, the tendency is to start mentally obsessing. The mind goes around like a gerbil on a wheel with seemingly no place to get off.

*To stop your mental obsession, you simply need to remind yourself that unanswered questions are just mental needs that the heart wants to meet.*

The multitude of unanswered questions and problems are only indicators that the heart is wanting to meet your needs. Ask, "What is the heart energy behind this question or problem?" Once the commitment is to the heart rather than to the problem, the problem will unravel itself.

Why would you want to step this heart system up a notch when it already works so much better than anything else up to this point? You may not at first, but remember, you are on a spiritual journey that goes beyond just you. Each one of us has a deep desire to be connected to the whole - the heart of the universe - God. You might confuse that desire with the need to have a lover in your life. That is not to say that having a lover is bad, but it might be like having coffee instead of protein when you need Endurance.

The "connect" we all long for is the connection to the whole of synergy. Synergy will literally bring heaven to earth. There will be no more struggling to make things happen, no more anxiety around relationships, because you *are* the heart of all hearts. The trinity of Power, Love, and Wisdom will come together within you and through you. All your needs will be met as never before because you will be more than you have ever been before. You will be all.

For example, you may have emotionally felt alone and so you went to your heart and discovered that your need was the energy of Community. You accepted Community into your life and, sure enough, things started to change. Some friends dropped by to chat, you were asked out to lunch by a co-worker. The immediate need was met, but the continual longing for that deeper connect was still there. To meet that deeper need, you have to go beyond your heart to the synergy of all hearts. Just as you accepted that your individual need was to have Community in your life; you must then accept that you are part of a bigger Community and allow that to manifest.

Does going to this bigger space make you fear your individual life will be out of your control? You might even think, "who is in charge of my life but me"? Since you are new to this synergy concept, you may have to remind yourself that you are no longer in charge; synergy is now creating for you. You now have the relief, the Support, the Power, and the sense of belonging that you have ached for deep within the core of your being. Your life is part of all life.

> *You now have the Power, Love and Wisdom of*
> *all living things.*

This journey covers another mile every time you birth one

more heart quality and accept it into your family of bodies. Instead of the bodies teaching the baby, the baby teaches them. Our whole inner family grows together. This is your exciting personal journey. However, it is not a journey for one. It is a group pilgrimage. Just as your four bodies must work together to support this growing up process, so must all people of the heart work together, through synergy, to create the ultimate spiritual journey.

## *A Prayer for Anyone on a Journey to Ultimate Spirituality*

I celebrate my life, the oneness of which I am a part. I celebrate the synergy of all Wisdom. The all-knowing, universal Truth, is mine. It works with me, and through me to direct every aspect of my life. I can now understand that the Wisdom of others is mine also.

I celebrate the oneness, or synergy, of all Love that is part of me; and I am part of it. From the space of Love there is no judgment; only Discernment that sees and accepts the real. From the space of Love I can also see the unreal but it never becomes my focus. As Love I can appreciate what Love others have in their lives because it resonates with me.

I celebrate the synergy of all Power as mine and me as it. I accept that this Power can literally change any and all things. Allies can be created in the midst of enemies. Abundance can flow while lack slithers all around. Cowards can claim Courage. Obstacles can become bridges, and dreams can come true. I now choose to support Power in others rather than be afraid of it; because they are being that Power for me, not against me. Amen.

CR

You are

on a

spiritual journey

that goes

beyond just you.

RO

| | | |
|---|---|---|
| Abundance | Flow | Patience |
| Acceptance | Focus | Peace |
| Adventure | Forgiveness | Persistence |
| Balance | Freedom | Play |
| Beauty | Gentleness | Power |
| Birth | Grace | Purification |
| Brotherhood | Gratitude | Purpose |
| Celebration | Growth | Release |
| Clarity | Healing | Responsibility |
| Cleansing | Harmony | Sharing |
| Comfort | Honesty | Simplicity |
| Commitment | Honor | Spontaneity |
| Communication | Humility | Strength |
| Community | Humor | Support |
| Compassion | Inspiration | Surrender |
| Courage | Integrity | Synergy |
| Creativity | Joy | Synthesis |
| Dedication | Kindness | Tenderness |
| Delight | Light | Transformation |
| Education | Love | Trust |
| Efficiency | Loyalty | Truth |
| Endurance | Nurturing | Understanding |
| Enthusiasm | Obedience | Unity |
| Expectancy | Oneness | Willingness |
| Faith | Openness | Wisdom |
| Flexibility | Passion | |

# Adawehi Healing Center Internet Classes

## Jackie Wood's personal growth classes are now available via the Internet!

Personal growth happens when your spirit breaks through the prison of hand-me-down patterns that you had previously assumed were your real essence. The birth of your real essence, or spirit, brings awareness. Your life can then be seen and felt in new ways.

Unfortunately, many of us believe that our hand-me-down patterns are real, and to give them up would be like killing off parts of our self. Since most of society reinforces this belief, it helps tremendously to have a support group that has birthed enough of their real essence to know their spirit can be free. The Internet classes can give you that kind of support.

To find out more about the
Adawehi Healing Center Internet Classes
visit www.adawehi.com

# Also by Jackie Woods

## <u>Spiritual Energy Cycles</u> (book)

This book has been described as "cliff notes" to all the metaphysical/self help books available now. It is a concise handbook on how to go about personal spiritual growth. Jackie teaches that you can discover who you are by what you create in your everyday life. If you are creating chaos in your life it is because of patterns that are blocking you from your full expression. For example, if you want Abundance or Love in your life, this book can show you how to identify the patterns that are preventing you from having what is rightfully yours.

## <u>Meditation and Needs</u> (audio tape)

Meditation is a journey into oneness; a place of true connection; a door opening into who you really are. Jackie explains specific tools to help quiet your bodies so that you can meditate and concludes with a guided meditation.

Needs are not forms or empty spaces to be filled. Needs are energies crying out for an exchange, and are gifts when you see them as signposts for the new energies you are needing to claim as your own. Jackie explains how to discover what your real needs are and how to get them met and concludes with a guided meditation.

## <u>Four-Way Mental Communication</u> <u>and Emotional Sharing</u> (audio CD)

In Part I, Four-Way Mental Communication, Jackie introduces a revolutionary approach to complete mental communication. This concept will help you understand your thinking process and also improve your communication with co-workers, friends, and lovers.

In Part II, Emotional Sharing, Jackie discusses emotional sharing as a tool that clears the space between two people and within yourself so that your heart will have an uncluttered place to express. This information is necessary for healthy living.

To order any of the titles by Jackie Woods,
call 828-894-0124 or fill out the form below.

You can also order online by visiting the
Adawehi Healing Center web site at www.adawehi.com

---

## ORDER FORM

Please send me:

_____ copy(s) of Spiritual Energy Cycles ($9.95 ea.)

_____ copy(s) of Meditation and Needs ($15.00 ea.)

_____ copy(s) of Four-Way Communication and
         Emotional Sharing ($19.95 ea.)

Name:

_____

Address:

_____

_____

_____

_____

Please indicate credit card:     VISA ☐       MC ☐

_____

Signature (for credit card purchases)

_____

Credit Card Number

Fill out the form and send check, money order, or credit card
information in U.S. funds only to Adawehi Press, P.O. Box 1549,
Columbus, NC 28722. Add S&H of $5.00 plus $1.00 per item
ordered. Please allow up to 4 weeks for delivery.